The Spiritual Tarot:

The Keys to the Divine Temple

By Marie-Claire Wilson

Second Edition

2013

The Spiritual Tarot:

The Keys to the Divine Temple

By Marie-Claire Wilson

First Edition

Text and Images

Copyright © 1992, 1995 Marie-Claire Wilson

Second Edition

Text and Images

Copyright © 2013 Marie-Claire Wilson

ISBN 978-0-9912135-0-4 (Paperback Edition)
ISBN 978-0-9912135-1-1 (Kindle Edition)

Dedication

I dedicate this book in devoted and loving memory to Mag, who often said to me:

"The most important thing in life is to be positive and constructive."

Mag opened my eyes and heart to the sanctuary of spirituality and for many years was my mentor in helping to further develop my intuition and work with the Tarot.

Thank you, Mag!

Acknowledgements

First Edition

I want to extend a very special thank you and deeply felt appreciation to Jeanine Normand, who not only helped immensely in the translation of the first edition of this book, but who also offered her friendship, support, and encouragement throughout that period in my life.

Second Edition

Many thanks and all my love to my dear spiritual companion and husband Scott. His ever-present love and support has encouraged me since the day I arrived in this country, more than 20 years ago. I sincerely appreciate his expertise and long hours in helping me more accurately express my understanding of the Tarot and spirituality within the English language. His own broad spiritual background and technological expertise truly helped me create a new and wonderful edition of my book. Without his help, this project would have never seen the light of day. This was our first publication working together; and God willing, the first of many more to come.

Table of Contents

Page intentionally left blank.

Time That Passes

21 years after I first brought the Spiritual Tarot to the United States, I am publishing the second edition of my book. To honor this passage of time, I would like share my poem with you.

Times that passes
Time that lasts
Time that is lost
Time that is bought
Time we give away and time we find again
Illusion of time
Emotion of time

Time that I would like to hold in my cupped hands
Time that has no refrain
Time that has sped me towards other heavens
Time that belongs to the temples of the gods
Time I wish would stop

Time that I would like to take me on its wings;
So that I can celebrate it

Time that opens my eyes to infinities
Time that makes me speak of coherent consistencies
But suddenly I wake up and so much time has passed
But I am always the same
Always seeking the crystal light

Marie-Claire Wilson

Page intentionally left blank.

Divinatory Arts in My Family

I would like to share with you my first connection with the Tarot and divinatory arts.

My great grandmother was a very well-known medium just outside of Marseille, France. As a child I was fascinated with the many people who visited her, with her crystal ball, with her Tarot decks and other 'tools of the trade', and especially with the rituals that she would perform by herself or with other women. My mother and aunt also have 'the gift' but they don't actively practice with it.

For a couple of years, while I was a young child, my mother took me every week to visit my great grandmother in her home outside of Marseille. (We lived in Marseille.) It was the most beautiful time of my childhood. For me it was a big event. I adored taking the old fashioned tram to get there.

I remember one day in particular when I was six years old. I remember that it was a day my great grandmother had decided to take off from her practice. During this visit, like other times when we visited her, she wanted to talk with my mother alone, so she asked me to take a nap. I never liked to take a nap! (I still don't!)

So this day she put me on a bed, inside a huge bedroom and closed the door. I wasn't the slightest bit sleepy, so I just looked around the big room. Time passed and I was really bored. I soon decided to explore my grandma's very big house. As I explored her house, I soon found her 'magic office.' The door was closed firmly.

But even as the small child that I was, with determination I managed to turn the large door knob, push open the heavy door and enter her special room. My gaze was first captured by the huge pendulum swinging in the corner of the room. I then wandered over to her desk and saw a strange looking deck of cards lying there. (I later found out that this deck was her *Tarot de Marseille*.) I then saw her large crystal ball and many other things that I didn't recognize at that time.

But the Tarot deck called out to me, so I picked it up in my little hands and started looking at all the strange pictures on the cards. Some of the pictures were beautiful, but some of them were kind of scary for the little girl that I was back then. None the less, I felt really drawn to this deck of cards, even though I didn't know what they meant.

Soon my great grandmother's voice startled me in the midst of my explorations. She said, "Oh, this is a funny way to take nap! What are you doing in my office?"

I meekly responded, "I am looking at your cards grandma!"

She looked me with her loving eyes and said, "What do you think about the cards?"

I responded, "Some of them are ugly grandma!"

She then started my first Tarot lesson within her comments that followed, "Yes, some of them are ugly. But it's not important how they look. What is important, is what the pictures mean, the pictures are symbols."

Of course I followed with, "What are symbols grandma?"

She lovingly and patiently responded, "These pictures speak to my intuition which helps me answer the questions that people ask when they visit me."

My endless questions continued, "Why do people ask you questions grandma?"

She responded with equally unending patience, "You need to know my little one that life is one big question. Remember this because some day you will be like me."

I will never forget this day! It was my first connection with the Tarot!

During another time when we visited, my mother and I were very impressed by how my great grandmother was dressed. She wore a very beautiful, long white silk dress and had white flowers in her hair. She told us that this day was a very special day for celebrating spring.

Later in the afternoon six other women showed up, each one wearing the same type of white dress, also with flowers in their hair. At five in the evening, they all walked out into my grandma's beautiful garden to begin their springtime ritual. They formed a circle, with my great grandmother in the middle. They then began to sing and chant strange words that I don't remember.

Another time, my mom and I were able to assist during a different kind of ceremony. During this ritual my great grandmother and all the other women wore long black dresses, with black scarves over their heads and white pearls in their hair. This was a remembrance of those who had died, sending love to those on the other side.

I was absolutely fascinated by these rituals and everything that my great grandmother did. She was unique and mystical in everything that she did. Yet she was grounded and realistic, speaking with clarity and directness. (As a small child, this made an impression on me.)

During our visits I saw many people stop their cars in front of her house. She spoke with so many people. My mother told me that some of them were very important and well-known in the community.

Unfortunately I didn't have the chance to spend many years with her, as she passed away when I was eight years old. Two months before her death, during a visit with her, she gave me her engagement ring.

She told me, "For your twentieth birthday, put this ring on your finger and keep it with you always. It will help you remember me. This ring has my energy and it will help you help other people someday. My soul will be watching over you."

At the time I was so young and didn't understand this very powerful message that she was giving to me. As a young adult, as I began to accomplish and practice with the Tarot, I finally understood the message she gave me so many years before.

This woman was really gifted and very special and I feel so very blessed to have had her as my great grandmother!

Blessings to you grandma!

Page intentionally left blank.

Preface to the Second Edition

The Spiritual Tarot looks at the manifest world as an illusion, as do some spiritual traditions. Most human beings live in this world of illusions; having been lulled to sleep with many distractions, fantasies, and false promises. As a person senses the inner dissatisfaction with these illusions, it becomes possible to seek happiness and fulfillment in other directions.

As the name suggests, the Spiritual Tarot is a spiritual journey of self-discovery, self-knowledge and self-mastery. This journey requires the spiritual seeker to look within themselves with honesty and courage.

This journey offers the possibility of learning major lessons about the nature of life. It is a journey to discover the reality of who we are as individuals, who we are in relationship to the Greater Reality, and to discover the true source of happiness, peace and inner completion.

The 22 cards in the Spiritual Tarot represent the major arcana and are archetypal or universal ideas within all of humanity. They exist within each of us. The major arcana relate to the three fundamental phases of existence: Birth, Life, and Death. Thus, the 22 cards in the Spiritual Tarot correspond to 22 major life lessons to be learned.

I have lived in several countries and have offered Tarot readings over the course of many years to clients of many different nationalities, cultures, religions and languages. Fundamentally, they all seek answers to the same basic human need – each person wants to be happy and live with happiness in their lives.

No one wants to suffer and everyone wants a 'place in the sun.' But how can we find happiness and peace in our life? These are the most basic questions of all, questions that each person will ask at some point in their life.

The chains of destiny are very heavy to carry around with us. The best way to keep these chains from weighing us down or chafing our skin raw, is to learn and apply a set of 'keys' that will open the doors to the 'divine temple', which is the sanctuary of spiritual development.

The Spiritual Tarot: The Keys to the Divine Temple is a book and Tarot system that will help you learn these life lessons as you develop self-knowledge, intuition and psychic energies. Each card offers a key to unlock the lessons of that card.

But as you begin this journey, it is important that you take up and appreciate the proper role of being a student, with all the humility and patience that this role requires. The journey will also require strength and discipline.

The spiritual path is not linear, but cyclical. After you have completed the 22 lessons in this Tarot system, you will find yourself coming back to the same lessons, over and over again. So it is with most spiritual disciplines. Each time we come back to the same lesson, we learn more of the details and nuances of that lesson and become better at it. Remember that obstacles are a common and necessary part of the educational process.

As you learn to see obstacles as opportunities to learn, you will gain new strength and unlock energy that will help you more effectively deal with the situations that confront you. As you work through these obstacles and move through the journey, you will come to realize that our mental outlook or attitude is really important.

Developing and practicing a mental outlook of being positive and constructive is vital to changing how we see the world and our efforts in it. That is not to say that we should become a Pollyanna with rose colored glasses, but it is important to set an obtainable goal and make our best efforts to obtain it. It's important to realize that thoughts are forms of energy, and that negative thoughts are forms of negative energy that will work against best efforts and deplete our store of energy.

But it's not enough to say "I want to" or "I would like to." Our will to take this spiritual journey must spring from the deepest part of our inner being and be borne from a genuine desire for success. We must stay constant and true to our course, avoiding the pitfalls of self-centered pride and egotism.

The 22 lessons contained within the Spiritual Tarot are meant to help you open the door to the divine temple within you. These lessons apply to our daily lives, our circumstances, our thought processes, and our spiritual growth. They are meant to help you become more skillful in life as you progress throughout your spiritual journey toward inner happiness and peace.

Once you begin the journey, never turn back or stop. Those who stop learning, who stop growing or who believe they have reached some pinnacle of perfection, will be lost, like the Fool that you will learn about in the Spiritual Tarot.

In this time of Aquarius, the worlds of the scientists and the mystics are intermingling together, as all begin to realize that they are looking at reality as two sides of the same coin. In the West in particular, we have held a notion toward reality that something is real only if we can see it (feel it, touch it, etc.). But I want to ask you to consider that just because something can't be seen doesn't mean it doesn't exist.

Even science these days has dispelled the 'seeing is believing' notion, as the boundaries of the 'unseen' have been broken and scientists explore the 'God' particle. They are coming to see and understand that there is a unified field of energy that underlies and is part of everything that is. The coming generation of scientists and mystics will work together to discover far more of about the nature of 'reality' than what we know now.

I wish you faith, courage, strength and awareness today, and in all your tomorrows.

Marie-Claire Wilson

Page intentionally left blank.

General Information about the Tarot

Generic Structure of the Tarot

In its classic form, the Tarot has 78 cards divided into two main groups.

- *22 cards forming the major arcana*
- *56 cards forming the minor arcana*

The first group of 22 cards consists of the major arcana, representing major life lessons in symbolically graphic form. Cosmic forces, the forces of nature, and the vices and virtues of humans are all represented in the vast array of intermingled graphic symbols.

While the major arcana are predominantly cosmic-level lessons, they operate on a practical plane at the same time. Many scholars believe that the original Tarot tradition consisted only of these 22 cards.

The second group of 56 cards is divided into four groups of 14 cards each, with each group corresponding more or less to the suits that everyone knows in ordinary game cards as clubs, spades, hearts, and diamonds. These four groups are known as the minor arcana and function principally on the earthly and practical planes. Many scholars believe the minor arcana were added to the Tarot much later in history, some estimating in the 1470s by French card makers.

The difference between ordinary game cards and that of the Tarot is of paramount importance. Ordinary card decks are for fun and games and can be enjoyed at public and social events, and are perfectly suited to such. The Tarot, on the other hand, is more or less for private use. The Tarot serves to facilitate the development of intuition for oneself, or having mastered the use the Tarot, one can work with it and intuition to help another person gain greater clarity about aspects of their life.

History of the Tarot

We don't know for certain the true origins of the Tarot, as it appears to have been in existence from ancient times. Some of the earliest Tarot systems that we know of were Egyptian and Greek. Adding to the difficulty in determining the Tarot's origin, many Tarot systems, from the earliest through more recent times, have been primarily oral.

As for the phonetic roots of the name Tarot, certain comparisons are helpful.

Sanskrit - TAT, which means all or total; and TAR-O, which means star

Chinese - TAO, which means the way, or wisdom

Egyptian - TAR, which means path; RO, ROS, and ROB, which means royal; TA-ROSH, which means the royal way; ATOR, which is another name for the Goddess Isis

Tibetan - TARA, which means Mother Goddess

Hebrew - TORAH, which means the body of wisdom and law contained in Jewish Scripture and other sacred literature and oral tradition

Arabic - TARIQA, which means the way, or wisdom

Greek - AORTE, which means vein or main artery to the heart

Latin - ORAT, which means she or he speaks

Spanish - ROTA, which means wheel

There are only a few dates that enable us to place the appearance of the Tarot in Europe. Depending on the sources consulted, you will find that there is still discussion and debate about precise events concerning the origins and development of the Tarot. The dates listed below are approximate and came from the Archives of Toulouse, France.

1376: A decree by the authorities of Florence, Italy, that prohibited a game called naibbe.

1377: A text by Friar Johannes, in Germany, mentioned a deck of strange cards that he'd seen in Switzerland.

1378: The arrival of the deck of cards was indicated in Spain.

1381: In France, the game/deck was quoted in some minutes written by a lawyer from Marseilles, France.

1382: A magistrate from Lille, France, enacted an ordinance against the card game/ deck.

1392: Charles Peupart, royal superintendent of finance for Charles VI, indicates that 56 sols were paid to Jacquemin Gringonneur of Paris, for painting three decks of cards in gold and gilt.

1450: Arrival of the VISCONTI-SFORZA TAROT, infused especially with Christian spirituality.

1457: Saint Antoine made a reference to the Tarot in his Treatise on Theology.

1500: The SERMONES DE LUDO CUM ALIIS, a Latin manuscript also called the Steele Manuscript, containing the list of the major arcana.

1761: Nicolas Conver, card maker in Marseilles, France, created the *Tarot of Marseilles. To do that, he preserved the woodcuts and paintings from classical engravers, and his work could be considered a faithful reproduction of the traditional iconography.*

1781: Court de Gebelin studied in particular the symbolism of the *Tarot of Marseilles, and presented it in "The Primitive World," Vol. 9. For this study, they employed one of the latest types of decks such as those made by Fautrier, who worked in Marseilles from 1753 to 1798. Nevertheless, Court de Gebelin made several errors in their graphic representations of the cards, for example, reversing the left and right arms of the Fool, and showing the Hanged Man reversed from the usual position. There are other errors as well.*

1791: A wig maker named Alliette under the pseudonym Etteilla (his name backwards) suggested relationships among the Tarot, astrology and kabbalah.

1889: Oswald Wirth, disciple of Stanislas de Guaita, published a deck of cards, in concept, close to that of Eliphas Levi, heightened with the Hebraic alphabetic letters.

1909: Dr. G. Encausse, under the name of Papus, published the

Tarot of the Bohemians and the Tarot for Prophesy. The English translator of Papus's work, A. E. Waite, put together another deck that was designed for him by Pamela Colman Smith, a deck much employed by the Anglo-Saxons.

1944: The philosopher A. Crowley put together another deck, published in the "Book of Toth," with the designs painted by Frieda Harris.

In all there are approximately 3000 tarots in the world today, in a wide variety of different formats, designs, and styles.

Introduction to the Spiritual Tarot

Twenty Two Major Arcana in the Spiritual Tarot

The Spiritual Tarot is a unique system that focuses on the 22 cards of the major arcana. These 22 cards call forth the most profound and archetypal ideas that are represented in all the world's great philosophies and exist in all cultures and all times.

Tarot systems from around the world reflect the many cultures and times that they been created in. For example there are Egyptian Tarots, Native American Tarots, African Tarots, French Tarots, mid- and far-Eastern Tarots, British Tarots, and so on. And there are some Tarot systems that combine elements from many cultures. Tarot systems also differ in form and format, but their messages are remarkably similar.

The Spiritual Tarot was created with the conscious intent to respect these universal source ideas as they originated in the earliest Tarot. Those ideas are portrayed here through powerful, classical Greek symbolism. The result is a system of Tarot where art, symbolism, and the initiation process all work together.

Classical Greek mythology is imbued with a long history of spirituality and philosophy. My spiritual roots are in Marseilles, where I was born. It is one of the most celebrated cities in France, and second only to Paris. During ancient times, Marseilles was the Greek port known as Massalia. That also explains, in part, my spiritual connection to the Greek Tarot tradition.

The cards that make up the Spiritual Tarot represent the many situations and 'rites of passage' encountered by the spiritual seeker who is on a journey to learn and practice. These 22 cards provide a profound and constructive foundation for posing and answering the many questions that the seeker may have. They serve as tools to help develop intuitive and psychic powers, and spiritual insight.

Each of the 22 cards contains a 'key' that will help the seeker open the gateways, one at a time, as she/he progresses along the journey.

How to Implement the Spiritual Tarot in Your Life

The Spiritual Tarot is a book and set of cards about self-discovery, self-knowledge, and practice. Some of the practices include meditation and the development of intuition. It is written for all those who wish to begin the journey. Pick up and work with what works for you and leave the rest.

Don't try to force yourself to follow a strict interpretation of something you may come up with in reading the book or cards, but rather allow yourself to follow what feels right, listen to the voice within you. We should apply ourselves in a progressive manner and in alliance with all the consciousness, awareness, aspirations, feelings, and emotions of the various characters of the Spiritual Tarot. This applies to the animate characters as well as the inanimate ones, since in the Spiritual Tarot, 'things' can represent 'beings.'

We can let ourselves go with the flow of thinking, feeling, and acting as these characters would, working with and through them. This process can help us to find the answers to what we seek. Often, those who practice the Tarot have come to appreciate the profound wisdom found in it.

Principles in Understanding Each Card

In some cultures, historical and present, people are not free to express their ideas, either in speech or in writing. In such circumstances, creative people often use symbolic words and graphic symbols to express their ideas but in a hidden form, the meaning of which is only known to those who can be trusted.

In ancient times, initiates of all cults always veiled their knowledge within allegories or graphic symbols that were fairly difficult to understand, thus keeping their meaning secret. Such was the case with the Tarot from its beginning and throughout all of the Middle Ages. The Tarot was a great mystery!

Accordingly, I created the Spiritual Tarot with two principles in mind:

First: To look for the most universal and elementary idea that comes to mind with the symbol. This central idea would be immediately evident, first on a subconscious level, and then rising into the conscious mind.

Second: To recognize the principal relationships that sprout from the fundamental idea of the symbol. When there is a web of relationships possible, you can choose those that afford the best connections to the main meaning.

Common Structure for Card Interpretation

As you begin to read chapter entries for each card, you will see that I have created a consistent framework for examining and discussing each card. The description of each card contains the following components.

- Card title and number (These also appear on the card itself.)
- A one sentence description of the central meaning of the card.
- A Key for the card; three brief phrases that contain essential interpretations that may serve to unlock the card's meaning within your particular circumstances. (A graphic symbol of a key appears on each card to remind you of the 'key' described in the book.)
- Skills to be Learned; three brief phrases summarizing central lessons to be learned from the card.
- Destiny of the number; a brief description of the destiny associated with the card's number.
- Numerology; a brief description of the numerology associated with the card's number.
- A large illustration of the card (Full color illustrations in the electronic versions of the book; black and white illustrations in the paper-based versions.)
- The General Meaning of the card.
- The Symbolism of the card.
- The Divinatory Meaning of the card.

Special Symbolism of the Halo-Like Auras

The halo-like aura found in many of the cards' images is similar to how the crown or halo-effect is often used to artistically represent the glow around the sun. This symbolism speaks to the solar origin of all that is sacred, celestial, and divine; and this often manifests as an aura. This aura around a person is a reflection of the radiating cosmic light that enters into the soul or heart center, where it concentrates. The light can then flow back out of us, to shine out into the world.

When the aura is shown around the head of a figure, it symbolizes spiritual attainment. When located elsewhere, it indicates the energy of spiritual attainment available as free energy. Two auras shown in opposite directions can be interpreted as complementary dualities, similar to what is represented as Yin and Yang in traditional Chinese philosophy.

The luminous cloud of an aura can contain many colors. In the card images, an aura is shown as gold and bright, with touches of other colors to convey diversity. The entire color spectrum facilitates communication, affinity, and alliance with the greater cosmos.

Symbolism of the Key for Each Card

In the description of each card in the book, there is a small section that contains the 'Key' for that particular card. The Key section contains three brief phrases that contain essential interpretations that may help you to unlock and better understand the card's meaning within the particular circumstances that you are involved in when you are working with that card.

You will notice that each card contains an image of a key, located in the lower right corner. This image of the key is meant to help remind you of the 'key' descriptions that are presented in the book.

Each card presents one key, offering the possibility of using that key to unlock the mystery of the lessons to be learned with that card. The cumulative result of obtaining all 22 keys is symbolically to pass the lessons of initiation and open the doors to the divine temple.

The concept of a 'key' also can remind us of music, where each key is a whole realm of particular energies, vibrations, tones, textures, and harmonies.

A 'key' can also represent a mystery to be penetrated or an enigma to be solved.

Another important aspect of the symbolism of a 'key' is that it can serve a dual role, in that keys are used for opening things as well as for closing them.

Page intentionally left blank.

How to Read the Spiritual Tarot

There are many ways that the Tarot can serve you. The most well-known reading practices include laying out the cards in specific formations, where each position in the formation represents an aspect of the subject matter, problem, or question that is being asked.

The Tarot is a system that speaks to each of us individually, in our own language, using our own inner voice. The Tarot will speak to you in a manner that is meant for you and you alone.

You'll get a lot out of *The Spiritual Tarot: The Keys to the Divine Temple* by practicing the recommended process that you will find in the pages that follow. As you work through these three successive reading levels, you may develop a personal bond with the cards that reflect life's important spiritual guidelines.

Some seekers who have followed this journey have developed certain intuitive skills that were previously undiscovered. Many happy surprises are in store for those who follow the journey of the Spiritual Tarot.

The Basics: Developing Intuition

First, make yourself at home with the images by studying the cards. What do you see in them? What thoughts come to mind? Do you sense any emotions connected to the images or symbols within the images?

Next, read and study the descriptions of each card in successive order, as if they were lessons in a course leading to a final exam about life. Contemplate the image of the card as you read its associated description. You may find it helpful to pause and meditate quietly for a time as you contemplate what you have read and what you see in the image. You may wish to take notes.

As you work through the process that is outlined in the three reading levels, you'll discover amazing connections. For example, it's obviously possible to draw the same card more than once. When you check your notes for this card, you may discover that you have similar kinds of thoughts and events each time you draw this card.

Finally, I suggest that you follow the three successive reading levels as described here, at first. Later you will become adept in reading the cards and may want to experiment with other methods. Later in this section I will outline another powerful method I use frequently.

This is your Tarot, your journey. Make it fun, and move ahead at your own pace.

Important Note: I suggest that you work with each reading level for one month before beginning the next successive reading level, during the following month.

First Reading Level

Begin on the first day of the month, or as close to it as possible. Ideally practice the following steps first thing in the morning, or at the beginning of your day.

1) Shuffle the deck, and draw a card.

2) Contemplate the image of this card and its description in the book. When finished, put the card aside and leave it out for the day.

3) In the evening or at the end of your day, write down in a notebook a brief summary of what happened during the day.

4) On the very top of the page, write down the name of the card that you drew that day.

5) In the top half of the page, write down the predominant thoughts, feelings, and reflections that you experienced during the day.

6) In the bottom half of the same page, briefly describe the predominant events that took place during that day, and how you responded to them.

7) Pick up the card that you left out during the day and contemplate it further. What correlations do you see between the messages of the card and the events, thoughts and emotions you experienced during the day? Write down your observations.

8) The next morning reinsert the card you drew on the previous day, back into the deck.

9) After reinserting the card, repeat the process in the same manner as described in steps 1– 8.

10) Continue this process for 22 days in all. Even though you may not select every card and some will be picked more than once, 22 days symbolize the 22 cards in this Tarot. So stop after 22 days.

11) For the remaining days in this month, take a break and leave your Tarot cards alone. It's important to rest between reading levels, to give what you are learning a chance to sink in. If you play 'goofy' with the Tarot, it will play 'goofy' with you.

Second Reading Level

1) Begin again on the first day of the month, or as close to it as possible.

2) Shuffle your deck, and draw a card.

3) Do NOT look at the card this time. Put it aside, face down. (Don't cheat and sneak a peek either.) This is so you won't have any preconceived ideas related to what may unfold during the day.

4) In the evening or at the end of your day, sit down and prepare for the exercise. DON'T LOOK at the card you drew yet. Write an account of your day in the same manner as described in the first reading level.

5) AFTER writing this account, now look at the card and study its description in the book.

6) What correlations do you see between the messages of the card and the events, thoughts and emotions you experienced during the day? Write down your observations.

7) Check your notes and see if you previously drew this card during the CURRENT month. If so, compare what you wrote today with what you wrote earlier this month.

8) Next, check your notes for LAST month to see if you drew this card. If so, compare what you wrote today with what you wrote last month.

9) You may find the correlations to be surprising.

10) Leave the card out for now and contemplate it further.

11) In the morning reinsert the card and repeat the process for the second reading level, using steps 1-10, for a total of 22 days, one card each day.

12) Stop after 22 days. For the remaining days in this month, take a break and leave your Tarot cards alone. Remember, it's important to rest between reading levels, to give what you are learning a chance to sink in.

Third Reading Level

1) Begin again on the first day of the month, or as close to it as possible.

2) Shuffle your deck, and draw a card.

3) Do NOT look at the card, but put it aside, face down.

4) In the evening or at the end of your day, sit down and prepare for the exercise. DON'T LOOK at the card you drew yet. Write an account of your day in the same manner as described in the first reading level.

5) AFTER writing this account, sit quietly in meditation for 10 to 15 minutes. Allow your mind to become quiet and don't think about anything in particular. Just allow whatever happens, to happen.

6) Do NOT look at the card yet.

7) Now look through your notes during the last two months. Compare what you wrote today with what you have written in past days. Do you find descriptions or accounts that are similar? What similarities or patterns do you see?

8) After this exploratory process, sit quietly and try to 'see' in your mind's eye which card you think that you drew this morning (Again – DON'T LOOK YET.)

9) Now look at the card and study its description in the book. Note how your personal interpretation with your Tarot is unfolding.

10) Contemplate all you have learned during the previous three months.

This is just the beginning of your personal connection to *The Spiritual Tarot: The Keys to the Divine Temple.*

Experiment after Learning the Basics

As you continue to practice, you will probably find that your intuition is becoming revealed to you more openly and easily. Here is an experiment you can try now.

First thing in the morning, draw a card and let the card speak to you about what you may experience during the coming day. Sit in quiet contemplation.

The message you receive may help you to see your way through doubts, dilemmas, and difficulties. You can also use this intuition to help you constructively plan for and deal with the potential of what you may face this day. Your intuition will continue to develop as you continue to work with the Tarot.

You may also enjoy laying the cards out in different spreads that signify specific aspects of a question or theme. There are many spreads that you can employ and many books that explain several popular spreads. You can also create your own layout as you begin to know the Spiritual Tarot as your friend.

The Four In Seven Spread

Another method of reading the cards involves a card layout known as the Four in Seven Spread. This consists of three rows of seven cards, plus the key card. You can apply this method to get a prompt answer to a specific question you might have.

Step One

1) Shuffle the Tarot cards.

2) Ask your question.

3) Shuffle the cards vigorously a second time.

4) Spread the cards out on the table, all of them face down.

5) WITHOUT turning them over, choose the cards, and arrange them from left to right in three rows, as shown in figure 1 below.

The Past

The Present

The Future

22nd Card (Key)

figure 1

- For the top row, select and place seven cards representing the past
- For the middle row, select and place seven cards representing the present
- For the bottom row, select and place seven cards representing the future
- WITHOUT turning it over, set aside the remaining card (the 22nd card) to serve as a Key to interpreting the message.

Step Two

1) Choose one card from each of the three rows and make a new row with these three cards directly in front of you, laying them from left to right as shown in figure 2 and as described below.

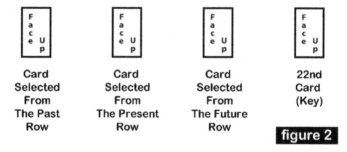

| Card Selected From The Past Row | Card Selected From The Present Row | Card Selected From The Future Row | 22nd Card (Key) |

figure 2

- Select one card from the top row representing the past. Lay this card face up in front of you, to your far left. This card identifies the elements forming the roots of the question.
- Select one card from the middle row representing the present. Lay it face up, just to the right of the first card you placed in front of you. This card indicates the present situation.
- Select one card from the from the bottom row representing the

future. Lay it face up, to the right of the other two cards you previously placed in front of you. This card presents possible directions or guides.

- Place the Key card face DOWN to the far right of the cards you placed in front of you.

Step Three

1) Look at the cards in front of you. If you need to, read the corresponding descriptions in the book to interpret the reading. In relaxed state of concentration, try to clarify your perception and understanding of the invisible energies of the Tarot and what they are saying to you.

2) You can also turn over the 22nd card if you want more details and a prompt answer. This last card can serve as a key to the immediate direction to take, or as a strong recommendation.

3) If the answer is still not clear, start over at the beginning with step one, and repeat the procedure.

If you want to ask another question, start over at the beginning with step one, and repeat the entire procedure. I frequently use this spread for my own questions and in working with friends and clients.

Page intentionally left blank.

Some Advice and Encouragement

The Spiritual Tarot: The Keys to the Divine Temple may not be the kind of book that you would read like a novel. But if you read and study it again and again, you will come to see and sense more in the card images, their characteristics and the messages they reveal.

From the infinite complexity of everyday events, guidance from the major arcana can help you find your direction and overcome obstacles of all kinds. You may find that the Spiritual Tarot can help you develop greater intuition and clarity. You may even find that it makes a wonderful nightstand companion and a good friend.

The study of the Spiritual Tarot is intended to intertwine with the study and practice of meditation and the development of mindfulness. There are many types or approaches to meditation and many organizations that can help you learn the techniques of meditation. There are also many wonderful books, written by truly skilled and accomplished meditation teachers that are readily available. Search, explore and find an approach to meditation that works for you.

As a word of caution, the Tarot has been misused by some as a shabby diversion or game of "reading the future." If you play silly games with the Tarot, you'll get silly answers. If you don't trust it, it will lead you astray. But if you earnestly work with and appreciate the Tarot, it will give you the maximum amount of help in your quest for spiritual growth. Awareness can bring the rewards of self-knowledge and self-mastery.

As a second word of caution, you may not want to loan out your personal Tarot deck to others. Some practitioners even go so far as to not let others even touch their personal Tarot deck. This practice of keeping personal objects, personal, is similar in many spiritual traditions concerning personal altar or sacred objects.

If you do let others touch or work with your deck, you may want to "clear the energy" with your favorite energy cleansing method, so that your deck will be full of your vibrations and yours alone. Some cleansing methods include swinging a crystal over the deck, holding the cards in incense smoke or simply holding them in your hands with the intention of clearing out all but your own vibrations.

Above all, don't forget that once you've decided to start upon the journey with the Spiritual Tarot, you will undoubtedly make some changes in the way that you view the world and how you react to it. You will also get to know your inner-self much better, both the "light" arrows and the "dark" ones as well. Remember the inscription written on the Temple of Apollo at Delphi, "Know Thyself." It is the first step of many spiritual pathways.

If you find yourself in a place where you are despondent and you feel a lack of power, look toward the horizon and a sunrise will appear. Know that the light is ready to guide you to where you need to go.

Remember: Happiness, Acceptance, Resistance, Forgiveness, Anger, Desire, and Love; all of these are possible experiences in life. Life is a choice, your choice! You are the wizard of your own destiny!

Card 1: Student

The seeker sets out to find the way.

Key for the Student Card

- *"Birthing" of awareness within the spiritual seeker*
- *Follow the "guiding star" throughout the journey*
- *Will to take action with humility and patience*

Skills to be Learned from the Student Card

- *Willingness to look beyond immediate circumstances*
- *Willingness to take responsibility and stop blaming*
- *Willingness to look within for the "dark" and "light"*

Destiny for the Number One

The destiny of the number one manifests as the heart begins to beat and is the fire of life. Development on our spiritual journey begins in the same way, as the Student has many lessons to learn in Schoolhouse Earth.

Numerology

The number one in numerology is the essential principle of everything. All things come from One and go back to One. Before One, there is nothing. The Universe does not have a beginning or an end. Everything in life is about this lesson.

The Student Card

General Meaning of the Student Card

The Student is becoming aware of the nature of the Greater Reality that underlies all that is, awakening to the Great Mystery; alert to the journey that faces all that seek this Greater Reality. Being a Student on this journey means beginning the process of learning to look at things differently. It means looking beyond immediate circumstances and letting go of the tendency to blame others (or God) for our misfortunes. It involves looking to see and understand the spiritual lessons to be learned within the circumstances offered in Schoolhouse Earth. This card signifies the initial phase of the "birthing" of awareness within the spiritual seeker.

We must first take stock of our personal inventory, both the "light arrows" and the "dark arrows" that exist within. And after making efforts with this inventory, we can then take steps forward to see and understand the experiences in Schoolhouse Earth that we need to learn in order to develop along our spiritual journey.

Symbolism of the Student Card

This card represents the Student beginning the study of spiritual wisdom. The cosmos gives us a "guiding star" that we must follow throughout our journey that is fraught with perils and obstacles.

The Student is wearing only a pair of shorts, symbolizing how in the spiritual realm, the cosmos holds little value for social trappings and outward appearances. What truly matters is the Divine spark that lies hidden, sleeping, within each human being.

Near the Student, you can see one of the first obstacles to be encountered: a rock blocking the path to the water. Water is absolutely necessary to life on Earth and survival without it is impossible. Drinking the water, a metaphor for drinking from the source of living Truth, is a necessity in our spiritual journey to evolve. Without water (spiritual truth) we cannot survive the journey.

Although the cosmos does not give the Student any protective clothing or armor, it does provide two tools:

1) A lance to protect us from the excesses of life.
2) A musical instrument, the lute, to enable us to communicate with the invisible Masters of the Universe, who provide access to the living

water. The lute also helps us to creatively solve problems.

The bright shining star in the cosmos above (and symbolically reflected on the ground below) guides the Student along the path. The energy from the cosmic star's shimmering vibrations serves to protect us and sustain our progress.

Divinatory Meaning of the Student Card

Being a Student on this journey means to understand that self-knowledge is obtained by a willingness to step aside from our ego and look within. It calls on our willingness to make consistent effort and accept perceptions that go beyond what is commonly accepted as rational - all with humility and patience. This is not easy because the ego has been in charge most of our lives.

Interpreting the card on an even deeper level, we realize through intuition and inner experiences, all life on Earth is interconnected and works together with purpose and competence. Love is the bond that connects us to each other and to all that exists in the web of life. Love through the cosmic Heart is the doorway to the awareness of this Great Mystery. We should be thankful that as human beings, are offered the chance to become aware of this Greater Reality.

We are subject to universal laws, even though we may not wish to think so. During our journey, we must acquire and apply three disciplines that reflect the larger universal design.

1) Aim (setting a higher goal)
2) Method (using appropriate means)
3) Monitoring (taking corrective action)

This card puts you, the seeker, in a position to acknowledge and begin to act on your responsibilities. You are ready to take action, yearning to be free. However, lacking experience in the situation renders you unable to actually get out in front of the situation.

When you are a Student, a beginner, new to the discipline, you must begin by listening and observing what happens, both in the world outside and in the world of thought, emotions and feelings inside you.

Energy and good will are here for you, providing you with strength in overcoming any weakness associated with being a "beginner." Mastery can be gained through your experiences and contributions, as time passes. Nothing is possible without these lessons.

The elements of success are there at your fingertips. It's up to you to implement them wisely, calmly, and with impartial and good judgment. Good judgment is probably the most rigorous of all disciplines we need to learn and it is also one of the most essential for our spiritual growth. Good judgment is especially helpful in avoiding the traps that are set by our self-centered ego and pride.

Don't let your ego or feelings of insecurity get in your way. Don't act out of anger or in a thoughtless, stubborn way, as these will not help you in your journey, but indeed will make it harder to understand the subtleties to be learned.

Being a Student requires two qualities that may seem contradictory at first: ambition and humility. Ambition is guided and tempered by the higher goal that the seeker has set (perhaps even unknowingly) and thus serves as the readiness to face whatever may be encountered.

Humility serves as the foundation in understanding that mistakes made in the beginning are a necessary and natural part of the evolutionary process. Mistakes along the way are inevitable. The key is to see, accept and learn from our mistakes. Consequently, it's necessary to reconcile these two contrary qualities - ambition and humility.

Take up the psychological stance of the Student with a willingness to make efforts and learn. However, be sure to remember diplomacy and avoid any impulsive or rash behavior.

Give yourself plenty of time for developing clear and unfiltered insight and vision into possible solutions.

This card encourages you to sustain this effort through faithful perseverance. Equipped with this perseverance and clarity, you must make efforts to keep the situation and your Aim clearly in your awareness.

Page intentionally left blank.

Card 2: High Priestess

She, who possesses wisdom and self-knowledge, controls all destinies.

Key for the High Priestess Card

- *Be aware of what is going on outside and inside*
- *Attune to the guidance that comes from within*
- *Work with the Divine Feminine*

Skills to be Learned from the High Priestess Card

- *Develop meditative practice to quiet the mind*
- *Listen to the voice that speaks from deep within*
- *Unravel outward troubles to reveal the necessary lessons*

Destiny the Number Two

The destiny of the number two manifests as the male supporting the female principle. The Yin and Yang of life is a beautiful reminder of the support and understanding it takes to have a loving relationship in family, friendship and with everyone in life, including nature and animals.

Numerology

The number two in numerology is a message of love, union, family, and friendship. This number is the union of two into one. But the number two also has other meanings:

1) Antagonism, in the form of confrontation and conflict
2) Movement and action

The High Priestess Card

General Meaning of the High Priestess Card

This card forces you to look within yourself. Faced with the current situation, you must cultivate and develop awareness of what is going on outside of you and inside you, with your emotions and thoughts. Your inner self and intuition are the keys with this card. You must have confidence in the cosmic forces, even though situations may seem insurmountable. This means taking in all of the elements of the situation so that you can allow the powers within you to do the work. Don't rush things; allow them to work out at the right time, in the right place.

Symbolism of the High Priestess Card

The card signifies the female element with receptive powers. The High Priestess, representing the Divine Feminine, is observing the destiny of the world from afar. The secrets to the mysteries are on a parchment at her knees.

The young woman's left hand, supporting her head in a pensive state, shows that she is busy with earthly concerns. The open position of her right hand represents her clear interpretation of cosmic guidelines, using her keen sense of intuition. These gestures together, represent navigating through the mundane by attuning to the spiritual guidance that is available, if you are open to receiving it. In order to be able to "hear" this inner guidance, you will need to learn to "quiet" the ever-chattering mind through meditative practice.

The young woman holds braced against her knee, a parchment that she is slightly obscuring with a fold of her gown. This represents the mysteries of a sacred science that cannot be taught, except to initiates. The parchment holds the key to open the door to a mysterious source of spiritual lessons.

We are seeking wisdom and solutions. At the same time, there are guidelines from the cosmos, which can come in the form of keys, as portrayed on the parchment. These keys, which can unlock such wisdom, can be found within us.

The High Priestess's face is framed by long hair decorated with a tiara. The tiara represents spiritual power over earthly concerns. The flowing veils attached to the tiara demonstrate that truth is not immediately evident for us on the earthly plane. The veils also indicate that great works are best created in peaceful concentration, and that that the process is helped by withdrawing into meditation.

The High Priestess is the mysterious, reserved, imperturbable, and deliberately hidden side of the female principle. She is seductive yet remains untouchable. She is the woman of cosmic intuitive knowledge and power; the wholeness of the Divine Feminine.

On each side of her, ropes represent the troubles we experience in this world: crises, dilemmas, and difficulties that we must succeed in unraveling. As we unravel these concerns, we can metaphorically prevent them from turning into heavy chains, whose links would chafe and scrape us to the bare bone. It's up to us to apply the healing powers of the High Priestess, to unravel these knots of suffering in order to arrive at a desired state of stability and tranquility.

Divinatory Meaning of the High Priestess Card

The High Priestess is reminding each of us who seeks, of the one question that is of utmost importance: the question of whether, in any given moment, we are Being or becoming. She is reminding us to **Be Here Now** *(as Ram Dass so poignantly wrote about so many years ago).*

Reflection and deep contemplation are necessary. You are obliged to complete the personal inventory you began as a Student. By searching deep within your innermost self, you can take an honest accounting of what you see, both the "light" and the "dark."

The solution does not come from an external source, or from what you see in the outside world or events. The way forward is perceived through a much more subtle approach to reality.

The solution will come through intuition and insight, even if this appears to be in complete contradiction to reason and logic. What you sense from deep inside is more likely to give you the answers you seek.

Card 3: Goddess of Love

Active female energy and universal love.

Key for the Goddess of Love Card

- *Love in action is the root of the creative principle*
- *Everything has its beginning, its growth, and its maturity*
- *Love is the protector, the transformer and the healer*

Skills to be Learned from the Goddess of Love Card

- *Open yourself to the gifts offered by the universe*
- *Learn the healing and transformative power of love*
- *Act with sensitivity, understanding and a positive attitude*

Destiny for the Number Three

The destiny of the number three manifests as the Pyramid of Life - mind, body, spirit - in perfect balance of the physical, the mental, and the spiritual realms.

Numerology

The number three is symbolic of the triangle and balance manifesting as creation, preservation and disintegration. Three is the essence of the soul - father, mother, and child.

The Goddess of Love Card

General Meaning of the Goddess of Love Card

The Goddess of Love represents the Universal Love that flows within all of life. She is a symbol of love's strength, beauty and protection. She personifies abundance, fertility, nurturing, good health, and prosperity.

Symbolism of the Goddess of Love Card

The Goddess of Love holds in her right hand a beautiful blue bird, symbolizing love in the form of a messenger sent from the cosmos. Her left hand holds a rose, symbolizing energy and passion. The symbolism of the woman holding a rose can also represent sexual mysteries and carnal passion. Together, the blue bird and the rose, illustrate the goddess's imperial, benevolent, and protective power she exercises over the world.

Her feet are resting on a pedestal, symbolizing the material world in submission to the power of cosmic love. Her throne represents her inner stability and command over civil order.

The circle of gold around her signifies higher consciousness, powerful intuition, and great esoteric wisdom. The golden circle is not closed for a good reason. She leaves an opening in the circle to welcome the cosmos to come and visit her at any time.

Her demeanor symbolizes womanhood in the more engaging form of the Goddess of Love incarnate. She embodies all the qualities of the High Priestess and the Divine Feminine in the preceding card, but here in a more active, instructive, constructive and positive manner.

The Goddess of Love has thus come to represent a "physical" manifestation of the priestess relating great spiritual power to the human and material plane. She is a spiritual realization or materialization in the earthly realm. The accent here is on the exemplary aspects of the exterior life balanced perfectly with the contemplative and receptive interior life.

The Goddess of Love is a symbol of strength and beauty, symbolizing that woman's love and energy are the root of the original creative principle: that all that exists in the world originates from this feminine principle. This is evident in the form of the primary trinity: the maiden, the mother, and the mature woman.

The Goddess of Love's creative and reproductive roles also extend into the esoteric plane, where her principal role is that of transformer and healer. A metaphor for this esoteric role can be expressed as the alchemist turning mercury into gold. The soft belt on her gown represents the male seed, whose existence can help her give and transform life. In this way, she can take base materiality and transform it into a fine, distinctive and spiritualized form.

Divinatory Meaning of the Goddess of Love

This card represents woman: the effective creator, the womb, the mold, the mother. She personifies universal and eternal characteristics that include abundance, fertility, a strong nurturing character, good health, and prosperity. She is also reflected within all that Mother Nature accomplishes, including birth and rebirth, as the archetypal mother. She is the eternal female Eve.

The seeker who draws this card can count on the active supportive energy of the Goddess of Love. The principle of rebirth means that life never really ends. Everything evolves, everything progresses, and everything begins all over again continuously.

The Universal Cosmic Mother watches over the evolution of her creations for which human beings are the intermediary producers and directors.

This card is particularly favorable for all projects in their creation or developmental stage. It favors conception, creation, birth, rebirth, good health, prosperity, and fertility. This card can mean a child is coming (be it literal or metaphoric), the development of a new project or career, or the occurrence of some happy surprise or event.

The seeker is guaranteed the supportive energy because the Goddess of Love brings understanding, expertise, and positive influence. You goal or purpose, promoted by active creative energy, volition, and will, is in the process of becoming manifest.

Card 4: Wise King

Act within the parameters of Universal Law.

Key for the Wise King Card

- *Conflicts and obstacles are part of the journey*
- *Will, planning and ethical action yield results*
- *The fruit of wealth and prosperity is often fleeting*

Skills to be Learned from the Wise King Card

- *Be warned, pride and ego will lead you astray*
- *Be guided by spiritual values*
- *Be open to the protection of Universal Law*

Destiny for the Number Four

The destiny of the number four manifests as the Foundation of Life that is reflected within many different cultures, in many different forms, all expressing various cornerstones for understanding life.

Numerology

The number four in numerology is an expression of the Foundation of Life: the four cardinal points, the four seasons and the four elements of air, earth, fire and water. Four is the number of realization, activation and implementation, as well as stability.

The Wise King Card

General Meaning of the Wise King Card

The Wise King possesses power, strength, and wealth on the earthly plane. But all can be lost if he becomes lost in pride and ego. The Wise King can accomplish much through careful consideration, willful and ethical action, guided by spiritual values and following Universal Law.

Symbolism of the Wise King Card

A helmet covers the head of the Wise King, symbolizing victorious power. In one hand, he holds a bunch of grapes, representing wealth and prosperity. But this prosperity is nonetheless accompanied by an ethereal forewarning in the form of a wavering veil, showing us that such good fortune is often fleeting and not really what we are looking for anyway.

The throne signifies the idea that anyone can accomplish their goal if they are willing to complete the labor required of such work. The cosmic scepter or staff that appears next to the Wise King is crowned with a three-lobed lily, also called the fleur-de-lys. This symbol also resembles the shamrock and the holy lily of ancient cultures. The lily and scepter are the symbol of benevolent authority, prosperity for the people, fertility, eternal life, spirituality, and rebirth.

The weakness portrayed in this man is his pride and ego. This weakness is represented by the agitation around this scepter, which stands ready to explode and destroy the protection it offers, if the power that the man exercises goes beyond the principles and virtues of Universal Law. Living within the worldly fruits of wealth and prosperity, this man of position needs the wise guidance of inner realization, perception, and compassion to remind him of his spiritual values.

Slightly to the left and above the seated figure, there is an eagle, a column, a figurine, and a circle. The eagle represents the will to help us move along our spiritual path, as well as the power to help us with our difficulties. However, when we grip such power, we must struggle to keep ourselves open to the simple truth that we must live in accordance with the spiritual values that are the bedrock of our journey.

The column represents the spiritual application of creative energies through physical labor in the material world. The figurine relates to the eagle, the column, and the circle as our responsibility to control the excesses of human pride and ego. The circle surrounding these elements represents the symbol of the higher mind that rules over the material realm for the good of all. It can also represent a shield, and joined with the symbolism of the helmet, it further symbolizes the eternal protection provided by Universal Law.

Divinatory Meaning of the Wise King Card

When you (as a seeker) receive this card, you may find yourself up against some rigid situation that may even be unsavory. It may also signify confrontation with authority. You must overcome your ego and insecurity; remain ethical in thought and action to successfully resolve the situation.

A struggle can be undertaken effectively because all supporting energy is there to permit a positive and constructive result. Before taking any action however, you must carefully formulate a well-planned strategy. Don't go off on some angry rampage even if you feel that you have strength in your favor, which is often the case.

In other words, even though this card represents strength, there are also the weak points of pride and ego. Pride and ego (sometimes stimulated by feeling insecure) always obscure our perception and the way we judge the elements of the situation.

First and foremost, you must rely on tact, diplomacy, compassion, and ethics. Granted, this is not always easy to do in everyday life.

The positive energy that is expressed by this card can lead the seeker either into strenuous battle or perhaps to realize a brilliant victory, all depending on your ability to learn to conquer your ego and pride.

Card 5: Holy Man

The one who has learned and lives spiritual principles.

Key for the Holy Man Card

- *Live with goodness, service and devotion*
- *Live in harmony with our brothers and sisters*
- *Live as an expression of love, beauty and light*

Skills to be Learned from the Holy Man Card

- *Find and enter the silence within meditation*
- *Listen to your conscience, to the voice within your Heart*
- *Live the spiritual principles and values you have learned*

Destiny for the Number Five

The destiny of the number five manifests as the Experiencer of Life, the five senses: sight, smell, taste, hearing and touch. It is reflected in being able to appreciate the wide variety and experiences in life.

Numerology

The number five in numerology is the physical number for humankind, also reflected in the human hand with the five fingers and foot with five toes. Five unites the four natural elements of Earth, Air, Fire and Water into a harmonious unity ruled by cosmic law.

The Holy Man Card

General Meaning of the Holy Man Card

This card represents a person who has mastered many lessons and accomplished high levels of spiritual practice. This person has learned to live a good life, treating others with love and respect, giving service and centered in the connection with the Divine. Yet to all observers, this person appears simple and humble, without the pageantry or the 'honors' of traditional religious station or rank.

Symbolism of the Holy Man Card

Sitting on a rock, the man appears plain and simple, but he conceals within his flowing robes, the essential truths that he has learned and practices. The rock represents the many mystery schools spread throughout all cultures and time. The robes symbolize inner conscience and self-knowledge. The clouds in the background demonstrate psychic talents and constant communion with cosmic and metaphysical sources.

In one hand the man holds the tablets that reveal the universal, cosmic laws that provide guidance for the spiritual journey. The tablets also teach us how to live in harmony with our brothers and sisters, through goodness, service and devotion.

The hand holding the tablets indicates mastery of the spiritual over the mundane. The other hand holds a candelabrum with three curving branches, set on a staff. The hand holding the staff signifies receptivity to the divine power.

The three branches of the candelabrum symbolize creative genius, inspiration, and the divine fire. This divine fire penetrates all the way across the three worlds: the divinely spiritual, the psychic or astral, and the physical.

These branches, along with the tablets, also signify a 'call' to take up the spiritual journey. This 'call' has been made from deep within one self, from the inner most center of our being. The card illustrates that the 'call' has been heard and heeded. It is the Divine 'calling us home.'

Divinatory Meaning of the Holy Man Card

Faced with this card you (as the seeker) must develop true conscience and live the spiritual values and principles that you have learned. Many spiritual traditions offer a simple but effective practice – "do onto others, as you would have them do onto you."

Live your life with beauty, thankfulness, compassion, forgiveness, generosity, humility, and sincerity. These are guideposts that will help the initiate live a life of meaning, purpose and in resonance with the Divine.

This card brings out the gift of inner knowing or conscience in you. It is the ability to listen to and hear the voice within your Heart. The inner most Heart is the doorway between the earthly plane of existence and the Divine.

If you can silence (at least momentarily) the inner talking and emotions of the self-centered ego and listen to your inner voice, your conscience, you will know in your Heart what action you must take or decision you must make. Your Heart will know, even though your head may not. Follow your Heart.

The 'call,' mentioned in paragraphs above, is the Divine speaking to us through the doorway of the Heart, asking us to open our Hearts to the love and beauty that is our birthright as a human being. By opening our Hearts, we allow love to flow within and through us, and out into the world. By practicing the principles and values of a spiritual life, we express the Divine's love, beauty and light out into the world.

Act in the world with strength and assuredness, with humility and patience, with love and generosity, all guided by listening carefully to your Heart of Hearts.

If you haven't yet fully mastered the skills presented in this card, use diplomacy, agreement, peace, compassion, and non-violence as your strategies. This is the indispensable stage where you must complete and carefully review your personal inventory.

It may be too soon for you to be capable of resolving a situation by yourself. Sometimes it's necessary to stand aside or to stay in the background while you permit a better-placed ally to come into action for you. Listen to your Heart to know when it is appropriate to take this approach. Your practice of humility can lead to a most effective and happy result.

As this card inspires your spiritual quest, listen to the inner voice within your Heart, heed its advice and have faith that this inner knowing will lead you in the direction that is best for you to follow.

Page intentionally left blank.

Card 6: Confusion

That which seems to be 'too good to be true,' is so.

Key for the Confusion Card

- *Be wary of outward appearances*
- *Be wary of automatic responses and reactions*
- *Be open to listening to the inner voice of intuition*

Skills to be Learned from the Confusion Card

- *Discernment*
- *Discipline*
- *Patience*

Destiny for the Number Six:

The destiny of the number six manifests as correct choice. Destiny reflects that building and maintaining the temple inside of you is in your hands.

Numerology

The number six in numerology is a master number; it is a symbol of perfect equilibrium. Six is two trinities (3+3) = the World = Star of David = wholeness, perfection and tranquility. Six is a number with the influence over the planet Venus, signifying an artistic soul with a big heart of compassion.

The Confusion Card

General Meaning of the Confusion Card

Life often seems to present us with a decision that involves one choice appearing to offer easy and quick reward, while another choice involves much effort and a just reward. Appearances can often be deceptive. Another message this card brings is that even though the right tools may be in hand, wrong choices can still be made.

Symbolism of the Confusion Card

This card depicts an indecisive man who has been placed between two women. The women are advising him about which of two possible routes he should take. The two women represent opposite approaches to decisions and the consequential paths that follow.

On one side, a woman offers the man intelligence, wisdom, and all the rewards that come from discipline, patience and practice. Her demeanor is strict, and the route she proposes is a long and difficult one.

On the other side, a woman, who is naked beneath her transparent gown, appears to promise the man grand results and pleasures with little effort. This route is meant to appear easy and enjoyable, symbolizing the snare set by illusions.

The two-edged sword and the shield shown in the illustration symbolize how careful thought and clear vision that can cut through the darkness of troubled times. These tools lie in the waiting, if the seeker chooses to use them.

This card symbolizes the conflicts and struggles that revolve around the choices between immediate satisfaction and long-term efforts that ultimately yield much more meaningful results. This antagonism signifies the struggle between emotion and reason, between superficial and substantive; a common struggle in most people's life.

This card is also about the temptations that arise in our quest for spiritual evolution, as interference can arise from countless distractions in the world around us.

Divinatory Meaning of the Confusion Card

For you (as the seeker) it's time again to honestly look at yourself and the decisions that you have made. You may find yourself faced with weighty decisions you must make. Guard against making choices that are based on automatic response patterns that have never worked very well anyway.

Beware of the illusion offered by the easy road, it is a trap. You risk getting bogged down on this material road, 'stuck in the mud' so to speak. There are no resources to call on for rescue if you get stuck in this terrain.

You must always be on your guard against things that seem too easy, that seem that they are 'too good to be true' – because they are just that - 'too good to be true.'

Your intuition can have a huge influence on which choice to take, if you are open to hearing its voice. The more that you yield to your intuition, the more it will help you to prevail in the decisions that you make. You'll recognize the right road to take because the solution will rise into your consciousness as some kind of sign during your meditation.

If you take what appears to be the hard road, a different kind of challenge awaits you. You will be tested through successive steps of liberation on your way to attain awareness and wisdom. And on this road, there is the help of those who have successfully taken this path before you. This is the best choice; these voluntary tests are a natural and traditional part of the path to initiation.

During our brief stay on this planet, we can learn to let go of our habitual ways of living and experience the value offered through spiritual teachings. This is not an easy task. Vice is generally more appealing than virtue. And the obstacles that block our road can at times seem impossible to surmount. These constitute the trials that we must endure through the initiation.

You will reap the reward or the punishment according to the choices your make. Remember that selfish desires acted upon without conscience, can cause harm to others and even more to you. Carefully examine your motives before acting on them.

As you continue the initiation process embedded with difficulties, remember that you are responding to a 'call' from your higher self. This 'call' is heard and understood by both your deepest inner self and by the cosmos. Don't neglect your 'call', or misinterpret its significance.

Guard against all the things that can make us deaf to the 'call': worldly success, pride, vanity, fame, glory, material wealth, and social rank.

If the lessons of this card teach you well, in the future you will know how to avoid the traps and pitfalls. The forces of cosmic energy are here at your disposition.

Page intentionally left blank.

Card 7: Realization

Progress has been achieved.

Key for the Realization Card

- *Effectiveness in action*
- *Positive results are certain*
- *Creative energies are at your disposal*

Skills to be Learned from the Realization Card

- *Establish and maintain order*
- *Place instincts and desire into servitude*
- *Master yourself*

Destiny for the Number Seven

The destiny of the number seven manifests as lessons from the forces of nature, deepening consciousness to obtain perfection. Anything is possible. As it is above, so it is below. The Divine is within humans, animals, trees, flowers and all that exists.

Numerology

The number seven is a master number in numerology. It is one of the most sacred and mystical of all numbers, because seven is the number of perfection. The number seven is found everywhere. Here are a few examples:

- The candelabra in the sacred temple of Jerusalem had seven branches.

The Realization Card

- Every seven months the body's tissues are replaced by new tissue, and every seven years all tissues in the body are completely changed.

- Seven is the number of the days of the week (in many cultures).

- There are seven chakras in psychic energy work.

- The spectrum in a rainbow is often represented with seven colors.

- The head of the human has seven openings.

- There are seven musical notes (in the Western musical traditions).

- There are seven tones to the human voice.

- The New Testament has seven sentences spoken by Jesus before he passes away.

General Meaning of the Realization Card

This card assures success for the seeker. The supportive energy from this card is profound. It accelerates your comprehension and perceptions of the evolutionary process, even including the most complex parts that are the hardest to understand.

Symbolism of the Realization Card

This card illustrates a strong goddess driving a chariot. There are three columns behind the chariot, and some figures on the chariot.

The woman is dressed in a tunic, the symbol of strength. This also represents discerning compassionate judgment, willpower, and action. On her head, she wears a helmet, the symbol of eternal light and sovereignty. She holds a sword and a shield. The sword is the sign of victory. The shield is the sign of eternity (a circle). The flower on the shield is the sign of divinity and the immortal flight of the soul.

She presents a beaming vibration that is the exaltation of intellectual power through the infinity of space and of time. She is standing, which demonstrates her active involvement and her vigilance.

She is holding out her free hand, signifying that she is in charge of guarding all of the order and rhythm she has created. She is also in charge of maintaining it. She is not bound at all by the physical plane, and she is much more attentive to and heedful of the spiritual domain, to which everything is connected.

The chariot signifies realization and implementation. It also signifies construction and reconstruction after the destruction of obstacles that were impeding or preventing evolution. The wheels represent a just and fair destiny. The chariot leads us down the road of light.

Base instincts and ill-conceived desire are subjugated symbolically by the positive spiritual energy pulling the chariot. This signifies the servitude of such base instincts and material things to higher intelligence. Higher intelligence also maintains the chariot and protects its wheels (destiny).

Two figures appear on the chariot, and their opposite shapes represent the harmony achieved by the victory. They both appear as receptive to the triumph that has been won over some significant ordeals, with great success.

The three columns soaring behind the chariot signify the will as it is victorious over all obstacles. They also signify victory over the three worlds: the physical, the astral, and the spiritual.

Divinatory Meaning of the Realization Card

This card represents the seeker who has gained entrance to and succeeded through seven gateways of initiation on the path of spiritual growth. The seeker has assimilated and profited from the lessons of the six preceding cards. Progress has been achieved.

Spiritual knowledge has been obtained. Your physical temperament, mental acuity, and spiritual aspirations are in complete harmony, all in perfect balance coming from your strong, secure, inner center.

You have control over your energy system. You have the ability to accomplish tasks on the physical plane. You can do it, so go ahead and try. You have leadership abilities at this time, as well as courage and a strong will.

You (as the seeker) are obedient to this higher intelligence and in accord with your own inner Aim. Higher intelligence must reign over the lower instincts and materialistic conceptions. Therefore you are not a monarch in the material sense, but rather governing as master of yourself.

The temptations of the mundane world have been surmounted, the body is under the control of a disciplined will, and victory is not the result of chance or mere luck. The methods employed to achieve it must be as ethical and as high-minded as the goal that has been targeted. Don't neglect anything for that. And, don't underestimate the adversary who knows how to set all sorts of traps very easily, including the very least expected ones!

Even if you think you're losing your equilibrium, keep up your faith and courage. You are assured that the hour of victory is very near. To realize it and to have it come to fruition, this is in your destiny.

Page intentionally left blank.

Card 8: Justice

Your future possibilities are bestowed by the actions you take today.

Key for the Justice Card

- *Whatever ye have sowed, so shall ye reap*
- *Accept responsibility for your choices*
- *Practice living in balance and harmony*

Skills to be Learned from the Justice Card

- *Awareness of your thoughts and emotions*
- *Awareness of your interconnectedness with others*
- *Awareness of order, equilibrium and fairness*

Destiny for the Number Eight

The destiny of the number eight manifests as the Evolution of Life. The lower material lessons of Earth are transformed into the higher spiritual dimension of power and justice. Focus your ambition in a way that is positive and constructive.

Numerology

The number eight in numerology is karmic evolution that transforms the joy and pain of Earth into the higher spiritual dimension. The esoteric meaning of eight is derived from $4 + 4 = 8$; where its realization results from the union of two opposing natures. Eight also represents justice and balance.

The Justice Card

General Meaning of the Justice Card

This card represents Justice as a fair, compassionate, and all-knowing dealer of cosmic karma. When you draw this card, you will be symbolically weighed in the cosmic court, with your actions and deeds on review. Remember, "Whatever ye have sowed, so shall ye reap."

Symbolism of the Justice Card

Justice, the woman who is pictured in this card, is uncompromising. She will apply the law without permitting any mitigating circumstances or excuses. This is the relentless workings of fate, the turning of the wheel of karma.

The radiating woman's face signifies that the power of Justice is incarnate. Justice holds two scales that represent the average weight of a human. Her scales are of fairness. These scales, when looked at from a distance, appear to be two eyes and they too, signify cosmic justice.

There is also a cosmic eye that is illustrated on the left, slightly below the angel's wing. This cosmic eye signifies that justice doesn't always take into account the social situations and social class of the guilty ones. This cosmic eye also symbolizes that the cosmos sees and knows everything, it is 'all knowing.'

This protective, unblinking, ever-staring, all knowing eye has symbolism that goes way back to many ancient cultures. The 'evil eye' (the eye of a person trying to hurt you) is the term for negative energy that is not related to your own karma, but that might be sent your way. This cosmic all knowing eye provides you with a shield to guard against that kind of negativity.

The angel's wing represents the light, feathery immortal soul of those who have lived a life of good intentions and actions.

Justice is riding in a boat that has a duck's head. This animal, in general, is always graceful in the water. But as soon as it tries to walk on land it becomes clumsy, symbolizing humans who are rather clumsy as they attempt to learn their lessons on Earth. This observation of clumsiness brings to mind a comment from Albert Einstein that roughly said - 'it is human folly to try to understand the mysteries of the universe through the intellect alone.'

Divinatory Meaning of the Justice Card

Justice is absolute in her responsibilities and obligations as she metes out karmic results. Beware, you can't escape (or be early or late in receiving) the cosmic justice that you face. She will weigh all the factors of the situation. She will see them balance according to the supreme laws: those of order, stability, balance, equilibrium, justice and fairness.

Disturbance of balance and harmony inevitably produces the reaction of Justice. And the inescapable result that she yields, good or bad, stems from the accumulation of your actions, thoughts and emotions. This is important because we are all interconnected within the cosmos: people, animals, the Earth, the planets, and the universe. If we wish to receive love, we must give love.

All action causes a reaction and people must know how to establish equilibrium among the forces that we release. We must be vigilant, pull out the weeds, and sow the best seeds. This is the hardest thing to do because we are confronted every day with the weeds in our own garden.

When you (as the seeker) get this card, you are coming into awareness about your place in the universal scheme of things. The power of this card protects those who are truly oppressed, and it punishes the guilty ones. Look to your conscience. We reap what we sow, for better or for worse.

You are moving to accept your responsibility for your past choices and actions. You may feel more mature than usual, blessed by a self-confidence directly caused by the universal will and natural law.

Listen and watch for a sign that will guide you to your next stage of growth. This will help you make it through a conflict of life coming to a resolution. You can feel your own peace returning. You have a new sense of yourself as powerful, moving through life with purpose.

If you're not feeling at ease, understand that what is happening is based on your past choices and actions. And for that, there are karmic repercussions.

Don't forget a few guide posts to live by:

- Do unto others as you would have them do unto you.

- Judge not, lest you be judged by the same measures that you apply against others.

- Compassion and humane actions are advised to keep focused on the surest path to spiritual growth.

- The esoteric principle of wisdom is inner truth.

- Remember that karma is about cause and effect; your future karma is governed by your actions today.

Page intentionally left blank.

Card 9: Hermit

Move forward slowly, guided by contemplation and keen judgment.

Key for the Hermit Card

- *Be alert, cautious and act with discretion*
- *Be true and follow your own path*
- *Be protective of your inner self*

Skills to be Learned from the Hermit Card

- *Deepen your contemplative and meditative practices*
- *Deepen your practice of humility and patience*
- *Follow your inner guidance and strength*

Destiny for the Number Nine

The destiny of the number nine manifests as the teacher of life, moving from isolated single mindedness to group consciousness. Use the discipline of a quite mind to find the divine voice within your Heart.

Numerology

The number nine in numerology is a master number. Nine is a number for great power, wisdom, independence, and inner solitude. Nine is the number of initiation in life. The number nine represents the Initiates and Pythagoras (who invented numerology).

The Hermit Card

General Meaning of the Hermit Card

Some of the traditional meanings associated with this card are: a sensible attitude, caution, modesty, and serenity. A keen sense of judgment also protects the seeker who is well-versed in ancient and universal wisdom.

Move forward slowly, cautiously and with discretion. Retire from the noise of crowds. Seek silence and serenity within meditative practices. Contemplative isolation is important.

Symbolism of the Hermit Card

This card presents us with a person of great wisdom who moves forward slowly. In one hand he carries and protects a lit lamp, representing knowledge and good judgment. The lamp is protected by his robe, which symbolizes discretion.

The Hermit probes the territory around him with the light of the lamp, moving slowly and cautiously. The light shining from the lamp is cupped by a fold in the sleeve, to keep it purposefully focused just where it is needed. This signifies that one should remain discrete, modest, and unpretentious.

The Hermit's second hand is pressed against the coat toward the heart, to represent the inner strength acquired through experience.

The Hermit is indifferent to the commotion of humanity, symbolized by the random vibrations of the column that is behind him.

A cosmic star looks out on the scene. The Hermit knows where he's going, guided and protected by the cosmic star.

Divinatory Meaning of the Hermit Card

This card is a warning for the seeker. You must go forward with caution if you want to outmaneuver the obstacles blocking your way. Don't make a hasty decision. Use your better judgment and the right choice will come to you. You should seek a retreat or shelter where you can serenely contemplate things. In silence and meditation, the solution that will resolve your difficulties or problems will come to you.

Contemplative isolation is an important lesson for you now. There are times when we must withdraw into ourselves, meditate, and concentrate on what is inside. This is how we get to know ourselves and the greater reality that is both within and without. What you seek is not outside yourself. It is within you, waiting to be discovered.

This is the only way that we can discover what our own, personal, true path is. It's also an excellent way for us to call upon the energy necessary to continue along our path.

Remember that if words are silver, silence is golden.

The experience gained from many lessons teaches the seeker how to be wise and protective of the inner self. Especially avoid fools who would pull you away from your spiritual path. Isolate yourself from those who roll around in the fantasies and distractions of life.

You can be solitary in a discrete manner. Seekers are advised to blend into the masses, to shun pride and remain humble.

The truth is not limited to a privileged few, nor is it relegated to a chosen time in history or a given place on Earth. All people, of all times, of all nations, can find and nourish the seeds of Truth that have been sown throughout all of history and within all countries and people.

Humanity itself, in whatever state it exists in, is the measure of how well and to what extent the universal mysteries have been found and taken up by those who live on the Earth. Many spiritual traditions say that to practice and live a spiritual life is in fact, the path to becoming what is a truly Human Being.

The Hermit is not interested in trying to enlighten the roiling crowds. He penetrates into the heart of things and into the souls of people, through silence, serenity, contemplation, and meditation.

Don't try to give the light to those who are not ready to see or ready to hear. If someone does not want to see the light, they will not see it. Their ego is still very much in command and it is afraid of the light. Those who are not ready to hear, will not hear and may turn the words they do pick up into vague explanations of a mirage they once experienced somewhere in the desert.

Reveal yourself to the world with modesty, through your kind and just actions. We should follow our own true path and by doing so, we may be able to help those who are capable of and willing to walk their own path.

The wise seeker is a humble master, totally adept at working with the forces from the non-material planes, those forces that are invisible. Retiring from the noise of crowds facilitates this introspective process.

This is why many spiritual traditions ask initiates to respect and practice in silence and serenity. The journey of the Spiritual Tarot is not an exception to this practice.

Be advised that a very keen sense of judgment keeps you aware of the cliff's edge and the abyss below, and so how to best avoid them. Let your judgment guide you in all your actions, even in the things that may seem unimportant. Nothing is too small to consider, for even the smallest pebble can make the temple of Jupiter fall.

Page intentionally left blank.

Card 10: Goddess of Destiny

Circumstances will continually present the opportunity for choice.

Key for the Goddess of Destiny Card

- *See beyond the enigma of current circumstances*
- *Carefully evaluate what is most important to you*
- *In your decisions, foresee the direction they will take you*

Skills to be Learned from the Goddess of Destiny Card

- *Be Mindful*
- *Be Present*
- *Be Here Now*

Destiny for the Number 10

The destiny of the number 10 manifests as the seed of perfection, rebirth and a possible new start. Destiny reflects through the gift of vision. Take courage and responsibility in life events.

Numerology

The number 10 in numerology is known as a universal and absolute number. The number 10 contains Being and Numbers, spirit and matter. In some spiritual traditions, 10 represents a complete number because it contains all the other numbers (0-9). Initiates say that every number after 10 is simply a repetition and addition; therefore there are no (unique) numbers higher than 10.

10 Goddess of Destiny

The Goddess of Destiny Card

General Meaning of the Goddess of Destiny Card

This card represents a test whose form, direction, and outcome are a function of the choices the seeker makes. The Goddess of Destiny watches over the ever-lasting question asked of every soul born on Earth: "Which direction will you choose in life?"

We can intentionally choose the path upwards, seeking the answers to the questions like … "Who am I?" and "What is the nature of reality?" Or we can by default, follow the way of the material plane and find ourselves on the downward path and attempt to find satisfaction through the fantasies and distractions offered by life. This card reveals to us a climate where the preparation of Destiny is unfolding.

Symbolism of the Goddess of Destiny Card

The symbolism of this card represents the descent of the spiritual essence into the earthly world (and all the materialism that it represents) and an eventual uplifting after that descent. This is the cosmic or divine journey of the One losing Itself in Everything, and then rediscovering Itself within all that is. Some spiritual traditions describe this journey as a cosmic game of 'hide and seek.'

In a similar fashion, this image represents all human life as we are faced with a lifetime of opportunities for spiritual growth, by working through the many lessons to be learned in Schoolhouse Earth.

The Goddess of Destiny is shown wrapped up in a tunic that signifies her inner powers. She holds herself still before the Wheel of Destiny. She keeps her arms behind her because she is allowing humans to direct our own destiny to our fullest capabilities.

The two figures struggling on opposite sides of the wheel represent humans in search of ourselves, pulled back and forth by contradictory forces. The figure that is approaching the Goddess of Destiny is awake and aware of what is happening and is prepared to deal with things as they arise. The other figure seems to be falling because he is 'asleep' in the grip of the ego and materialism it lives in.

The eternal lesson of the Wheel of Destiny, without beginning or end, expresses an aspect of karma. It is the wheel of life in all our existences, in this life and in former lives, up to the final purification, when all of our mistakes and their consequences have played out.

Sometimes this card depicts irony and a state of instability. In this interpretation, succeeding to a higher level is dependent on your personal achievement and effort, so that future success or failure is yet unknown. But evolution is always possible with the Goddess of Destiny by your side.

After undergoing the sacrifices we must and passing the tests offered through our lessons, we become more aware and are liberated by Destiny. This happens when we finally understand the illusion of the manifest world and we firmly set our aim to live our lives in concert with the divine symphony of the universe.

Divinatory Meaning of the Goddess of Destiny Card

Destiny provides three equations to be solved by everyone who enters the Wheel of Life: there are the events we must live through, the suffering that unavoidably goes with these events and the possibility of changing experiences yet to come by changing the nature of how we perceive the world and the greater Reality that surrounds and is within it.

The Wheel of Destiny shows us that we are all caught in the patterns of our life as long as we continue to live our lives in a state of waking or walking 'sleep.' In this state of 'sleep' we do not know the Greater Reality that exists beyond our 'prison' walls, we are unconscious and chained to our blind passions and aversions, suffering incessantly, it would seem.

We must learn to more accurately perceive the enigma of our lives in the face of what may appear to be arbitrary, intentional, or unfair obstacles, crises and life events. We must learn to see beyond the pain and circumstances of the situations so that we can perceive, understand and act on the lessons about ourselves (our attachments, aversions, conditioned patterns, etc.) and about our true nature and how it relates to the Great Mystery.

Events represent constant action and adaptation, with more or less ease, to the situations presented in everyday life. The events of our lives offer us the opportunity to learn and grow, or we can succumb to the test and experience nothing but the pain and suffering of the situation.

Freedom can only come from a change in the way we perceive the situation, with awareness and presence. The more we are aware, the freer we become; not to change events, but to shape our reactions to those events. When we can 'see' with this kind of perception, we experience Destiny as brining to us what is needed in order to learn to find the peace and freedom that we seek.

It is important in everyday life to always live as mindfully as possible, by being present in the moment. Do not be pulled into the past, with all its second-guessing and regrets. And do not yearn for future situations that may or may not take place. If you are living in the past or living in the future, you really aren't here are you?

Be Here Now.

Page intentionally left blank.

Card 11: Cosmic Power

One who has gained self-mastery of the ego and life's temptations.

Key for the Cosmic Power Card

- *Dynamic cosmic power and protection*
- *Self-mastery of the ego and the temptations of life*
- *Action in a gentle, positive and constructive way*

Skills to be Learned from the Cosmic Power Card

- *Compassion and inner strength*
- *Fairness and equity*
- *Integrity and faith*

Destiny for the Number 11

The destiny of the number 11 manifests as psychic powers and material might, revealing new perspectives, charisma and artistic talents. Listen to your inner voice to find your mission.

Numerology

The number 11 in numerology represents going beyond the limits and boundaries and passing from one realm to another. 11 is a number for power and strength. The number 11 suggests that you face the challenges of life with a strong attitude. $1 + 1 = 11$ illustrates the idea that the number 11 consolidates.

The Cosmic Power Card

General Meaning of the Cosmic Power Card

This card signifies that all the necessary elements are present and within your reach to escape from whatever situation is holding you back. When you draw this card, you can be assured that dynamic cosmic power and protection reflects on you. Remember to stay in control of any impulse to become overly dominating, and you will surely be victorious.

Symbolism of the Cosmic Power Card

This card shows that a young woman has formed an alliance with both a lion and with serpents. She is able to do this due to her self-mastery of the ego and the many temptations of life. She acquired her self-mastery through self-knowledge, letting go of attachments and aversions and opening her heart to the cosmic power that resides within the inner Heart of every human being.

This woman who represents cosmic power may appear on the surface to be weak and defenseless, but she has great inner strength and manifests a strong positive force in the world. The gentleness of the womanly character reflects supreme power as both receptive and productive. She is unarmed, without weapons or shields, to demonstrate that her inner and spiritual energies are superior forces.

She holds out her arms, gazing with intense concentration. Her stance in this way reveals that it is by the sheer nature of her deep connection to goodness, equity, fairness, integrity and compassion that she holds the lion and the serpents mesmerized in total respect for her.

Her 'way of being', the manner of how she lives in the world, is one of kindness, compassion, and illustrates her positive and constructive nature in all that she does.

The lion symbolizes the sun, the fire of purification, and the great strength of the cosmic power of love.

The serpents symbolize the power of spiritual attainment achieved through sacred wisdom applied fairly and with wise judgment.

The cosmic star soars above and radiates positive energy to protect the young woman.

Divinatory Meaning of the Cosmic Power Card

This card expresses the high spiritual attainment of the seeker who has cleared away the inner debris and has opened the connection to cosmic power through the threshold of the inner Heart.

The higher mind (inner Heart) is what motivates the universe as the original power from which all other powers are born. By clearing away the veils of the earthly plane, the young woman has opened herself to becoming an open conduit for the ever flowing cosmic power.

The woman represents the supreme and creative forces of Mother Nature, inextricably linked with the ever-present energy of cosmic power. Through her inner strength, endurance and persistence, this young woman has easily tamed the lion and the serpents. She manifests her inner strength through her positive and constructive way of experiencing the world and all in it, including animals.

The person illustrated here is a woman of faith, but not in the sense that many people use the word faith. We don't mean blind faith where one simply takes what is written in scripture or the word of another, as true in and of itself.

Faith can be described as beginning with a continually growing 'data-base' of intellectual knowledge concerning the nature of the Greater Reality. This involves searching for truth in an open, honest and unfiltered manner, with a willingness and desire to look into many different and varied sources.

But faith only begins with this wide base of intellectual knowledge. True faith is developed as one continues along the spiritual journey with personal experiences that might be expressed as glimpses, brief connections, or reflections of the cosmic love that is within every Heart. One continues the journey of faith by opening one's inner Heart to the experience of cosmic love.

The seeker is reminded of faith when things become bogged down in false pride, jealousy, and egotism; and when materialistic concerns obscure the good and just life. This doesn't mean that you should reject material concerns or to try and shun the world we live in. Rather, you would be wise to gently participate in the matters of life without becoming stuck in its mud, memorized, only to forget your greater calling.

Don't be afraid of failure because nothing ventured, nothing gained. We learn from our mistakes, so we must brave the risks. And beware that doubt or fear may act like the straw that breaks the camel's back. So go forward with courage, this card supports you in your efforts.

This card can also counsel you about the cosmic plan if you ask for it. The amount of cosmic support and the amount of labor required to mitigate the effects of hardships and tribulation is all in direct proportion to the true faith of the seeker.

Page intentionally left blank.

Card 12: Hanged Man

One must die (in a symbolic way) in order to live an authentic life.

Key for the Hanged Man Card

- *What now seems to be sacrifice, may later be seen as achievement*
- *Give up self-centeredness to gain universal connectedness*
- *Seek harmonious balance between material and spiritual realms*

Skills to be Learned from the Hanged Man Card

- *Self-knowledge through the discipline of inner work*
- *Knowledge of Self in relationship to the Great Mystery*
- *Bring your lower self in servitude of your higher self*

Destiny for the Number 12

The destiny of the number 12 manifests as sacrifice and the death of the self-centered ego. Remember that hesitation, non-acceptance and resistance are obstacles in moving forward toward becoming free.

Numerology

The number 12 in numerology represents the cosmic work that has been accomplished. 12 is the number for the cosmic system of government. It can be related to the 12 signs of the Zodiac and the 12 months in the Gregorian calendar. This number has a special spiritual significance in life because it indicates that we don't have much choice and are stopped in what we are doing, be it for the good or for the bad. 12 is a number of sacrifice and suffering for a cause that is not necessary noble. 12 is a difficult number to deal with.

The Hanged Man Card

General Meaning of the Hanged Man Card

This card symbolizes the seeker who must willingly accept the sacrifice (taming) of the self-centered ego and who must die in a symbolic way, to the false promises and powerful illusions of the outer world. The seeker must accomplish this in order to live an authentic inner life with purpose.

Symbolism of the Hanged Man Card

This card illustrates a man with his arms tied behind his back. He's hanging by one foot attached to the gallows, braced atop two standing columns. But in this card, the hanged man is not a criminal, he is a seeker.

The hanged man represents the death (taming) of the self-centered ego. The lesson here is that you must let go of the grip of the ego in order to experience a much deeper sense of who you really are and who you are in relationship to the Great Mystery.

The hanged man also represents letting go of painful situations.

The legs tied up as they are, signifies atonement, the good that results from a painful lesson. Part of life is the experience of pleasure and pain, not as a reward or punishment, but to provide a context, a 'schoolhouse' in order to help us learn the lessons we have to learn.

The feet and hands, in many spiritual and healing traditions, are seen as powerful receptors of energy. The hanged man, with feet turned toward heaven, is drawing in the cosmic force of the universe through his feet. The figure is inactive in a bodily way, although it is evident by the energy radiating from his head that he is receiving and being strengthened by cosmic energy.

Above the gallows, the cosmic eye protects the hanged man. The cosmic eye also represents intuition in this illustration. The unblinking cosmic eye is glowing in the vibrant pyramid of cosmic destiny.

On each side of the image you can see the columns with greenery trailing up along them, signifying the harmony between material and spiritual realms, when the seeker learns to live in a state of balance.

Divinatory Meaning of the Hanged Man Card

When encountering this card you (as the seeker) may be in a state of awe, more or less. You have a cellular memory of a calling from far, ancient memories that may have been forgotten in your present form.

When the inner cosmic call breaks through into your current state of consciousness by means of strong or irresistible feelings (intuition), you are advised to seek silence and solitude to facilitate this communion. This type of communication is an inner and private experience that is not well suited for expression in words or on an intellectual plane.

This card represents your secret garden; you have the only key. The courage to sacrifice the desires of the self-centered ego, to give up that part of you that is stuck in materialism and the illusion of false reward (money, power, fame, etc.) represents a major guidepost along most esoteric spiritual paths.

A key is self-knowledge and finding methods for taming the ego. Turn inward and observe its many faces, voices, songs, and stories; they are all patterns that play out in our lives, over and over. We learn these patterns as very young children, many from our parents and some may come from other lifetimes.

You must develop acceptance of the patterns which you see within you and acceptance of the external circumstances as they are. Don't blame others (or God) for the harsh circumstances you may find yourself in. It is your choice in how you perceive and work with the situation, as the hanged man. Do not complain and play victim, but take responsibility and take wise action. If you are sincere, there are tremendous benefits to be gained.

To conquer the self-centered ego is to know that you are not separate from anyone else. What you see in someone else, is within you. We are all a part of the great cosmos, the interconnected web of life, in intimate ways we can never understand fully.

You must realize that as a human being born on Earth, we are subject to cosmic forces in play. The ordeals that we face in life are necessary exercises in which we learn important lessons. This not only pertains to accepting sacrifice on whatever material level is necessary, but more importantly, to accepting an important change that you will need to make in order to reach within your deepest, innermost self.

This is not only a change to inform you, but a change that can affect dramatic progress in your spiritual journey. All of this requires a crucial struggle to bring your rational mind and your self-centered ego into the servitude of your higher self.

I am reminded that we are born alone, we live alone, we die alone and we are always alone with our thoughts. Yet if we learn to still the mind, we may find ourselves able to open to the universal cosmic web that connects everyone and every living thing.

This card signifies that everything appears to be turned upside down and drastically changed. Dramatic reversal in situation refers to the impression that you have gone through the mirror to the other side of reality. What once seemed rational and logical now seems upside down. Step back and attempt to view circumstances from a larger perspective. Do you sense a voice from deep within?

Confronted with others, confronted with the situation, confronted with new ideas, you will have to show yourself worthy and not give in to hasty or compromising acceptance just because you may want the easy way out. There may be a sacrifice to make. Have the courage to rise to the situation.

Sacrifice is a law that rules throughout all creation, and we must not expect any reward from our sacrifices. This passive yet required renunciation will allow you to follow the natural flow of the universe, using whatever you encounter to help you grow.

Several great prophets and leaders have met suffering in their lives, sometimes with tragic ends; Jesus, Muhammad, Gandhi, Dr. Martin Luther King and many others.

This card also represents the strength and valor of a person who attempts to communicate a message essential to the collective human evolution. The hanged man symbolizes the many wise men and women who would die in the pursuit of truth.

The hands tied behind the back symbolizes the reality that ideas live on, surviving those who sacrifice themselves and that these ideas will be inherited and harvested by others who will expand on them at the right time.

All of the wise men and women, who have come before, have left legacies of their teachings and paths to follow. They gave their lives as a gift to humanity so that future generations might continue the challenge of learning what it is to become a truly Human Being.

Those of this century must continue this work, passing on what has been learned from one generation to the next, from one time to another, for eternity.

Card 13: Transformation

Transformation of the old soon yields buds in the garden.

Key for the Transformation Card

- *Dramatic transformation, perhaps internal, perhaps external*
- *"Spring cleaning" of old ways, perceptions and patterns*
- *Cleansing soon brings new freedom, vision and understanding*

Skills to be Learned from the Transformation Card

- *Discern what is of value and that which is not*
- *Discern lessons to be learned in present circumstances*
- *Accept change with a positive and constructive attitude*

Destiny for the Number 13

The destiny of the number 13 manifests as the reality of life, the need to deal with constant change. Transformation is the only constant. Experiences in life are like every minute on a clock, here for the moment, gone the next. Accept this reality.

Numerology

The number 13 in numerology is a number that represents necessary outcomes and the mandatory transformation of all that exists.

The Transformation Card

General Meaning of the Transformation Card

This card in many Tarot systems represents death of some kind, be it symbolic as it is in most cases, or in rare circumstances even the death of the actual physical body. But in the Spiritual Tarot (and many other systems as well) the most significant aspect of this card is that it represents a dramatic change in direction, a powerful transformation of some type for the seeker or someone close to the seeker. All of these interpretations are generally followed by the assurance that the beginning of the next cycle is close at hand, or that the birthing of a new phase is near.

Symbolism of the Transformation Card

The central image in this card is an hourglass, the infinitely reversible timekeeper, showing us that the end of one era transforms cleanly into the next era, as the now empty bottom of hourglass is turned over to yield a new beginning and a new cycle.

The two vertical serpents on either side, which are holding up the cosmic hourglass, represent a 'holding at bay' of the commotion and distractions of this world.

In the upper left of the hour glass, you can see that the warrior has taken off his officer's helmet and medals in order to be able to slip through the narrow opening in the hourglass passage. This shows that he knows that his medals won't mean much where he is going. And he also knows that his shield of honor and warrior's weapons won't protect him anymore either.

Keeping the soldier company is a lion, the symbol of spiritual and physical strength, an important quality of character during this powerful transformational phase. There is also a bottle containing human ashes that will forevermore be a part of human destiny.

Divinatory Meaning of the Transformation Card

When you (as the seeker) draw this card, you can expect a complete and radical change in your situation. This card heralds an unforeseen renewal that is ultimately in your favor.

Sometimes there is a harsh and maybe even ruthless change in direction, which can be painful. And yet if this same event is perceived in another light, it might be seen as healing. What follows may be the announcement of a happy occurrence, such as the beginning of a new relationship, a new career, or a new direction. All of this can suggest that such new and dramatic occurrences happen when you've reached the end of something old that is no longer well-suited for you.

This card signals that you must cleanse your psyche of old business, such as fears and blockages, and old ways of perceiving the world. This psychic cleansing takes place more effectively in silence and meditation.

With this card there is also the strong implication and suggestion that you accept this change and cleansing with a proper attitude. You have outgrown your old skin, so you shed it and grow a new one. An old pattern is being replaced by a new and mindful path forward.

And with this cleansing will come a new freedom, a new vision, and a new understanding. If the transformation is accomplished with a positive attitude, the spirit is freed to work toward spiritual attainment with renewed vigor.

As mentioned previously, death is often associated with this card. Many people, especially in the West, want to push off and try to forget about the reality that death will someday come knocking on their door. Death is the moment most of us fear the most. Yet death is an inevitable part of the life cycle, it is one of the three basic cosmic laws of certainty: birth, growth and death.

Many spiritual traditions speak of other ways of understanding the nature of life and death. On a deeper level, knowledge of our true self and our relationship to the Great Mystery may allow the seeker to gain an expanded appreciation of 'what lives', 'what dies' and 'what remains'. Several yoga masters have reflected about these questions and have been quoted as saying:

"I am not this body. I am not this mind. I am not these emotions. I Am."

So how does the above quote fit with your understanding and relationship to the idea of death? You may wish to contemplate this.

This card is not about destruction, but it is about transformations which can teach us very valuable lessons. The seeker must 'die' in the profane world in order to be 'born' into the spiritual life.

With spiritual transformation, one must leave the old state of imperfection to rise above and begin something new. This pseudo-death and rebirth is represented within most traditions of initiation.

You may think that you will be stuck in this 'dying place' forever if you cannot see beyond it. But don't let it get you down, even if it's hard to keep moving or if you feel like you are walking through quicksand. Get on the path of awareness and let go of the outmoded, the useless and the destructive. Welcome the new.

The passage of time will show you the wisdom and necessity of transformation. It will be difficult and painful, but you will soon see that it is for the best.

Page intentionally left blank.

Card 14: Moderation

Fluidity comes through the middle path of moderation and not by taking up the extremes.

Key for the Moderation Card

- *Bring light into the dark areas you avoid*
- *Bring your ego into your house as a servant*
- *Bring balance into the solutions you seek*

Skills to be Learned from the Moderation Card

- *Determine what is needed and appropriate*
- *Distinguish the container from the contents*
- *Practice harmony within yourself and with others*

Destiny for the Number 14

The destiny of the number 14 manifests as harmony and peace; everything in the right place at the right time.

Numerology

The number 14 in numerology represents a person holding and acting with the attitude that is appropriate in any given situation. This number acts as a diplomat, behaving with respect, skill and harmony. The number represented as 7 + 7 = 14, symbolizes the perfect union on the inner plane, the perfect regenerative union as the essence of life.

The Moderation Card

General Meaning of the Moderation Card

Two of the central symbols within the illustration are the water bearer and the vase she will carry. The Greek word Hydrochoos (later translated as Aquarius) means the person who is the water bearer or water carrier. Traditionally, Hydrochoos personifies temperance, sobriety, moderation, and self-control. The deeper aspects of these qualities include abstinence, denial, forbearance, and making amends or atonement when necessary.

Symbolism of the Moderation Card

This card portrays a woman magician or priestess, who is bearing water (living truth) to all of humanity. The illustration of the brilliant light, or sun above her, represents cosmic splendor and the nature principal in all of its life forms.

The priestess is protected and inspired by the cosmic energy that is flowing down from the sun. Her appearance is androgynous because she represents the collective humanity, not an individualized person. She is an expression of universal fluidity. The fluidity comes from taking the middle path of moderation and not taking up any of the extremes.

The cosmic spirit of the sun is pouring water out of the 'well of life' into the urn on the ground. The well of life contains the water (essence) of universal life that is poured into this earthly plane from the cosmic plane. The water is contained so that it can be given where needed. Again, an expression of moderation in doing what is appropriate, where appropriate.

If you look closely you can see a butterfly on the urn. It symbolizes the seven chakras in peace and harmony.

Divinatory Meaning of the Moderation Card

When you (as the seeker) draw this card, you are being shown the well of life representing the many lessons, purifications, and transformations that are required of all of us who would evolve. It involves the taming (not the destroying) of the self-centered ego for the good of our inner self. Again, this is a revelation of moderation, as we learn to bring the ego into the house as a servant, so that it may serve the needs of the master of the house (your inner self).

You are being granted psychic receptivity to find your balance and the solutions you seek. You need to know how to distinguish the container from the contents within it. Or said another way, not judge a book by its cover. This is an important lesson to learn.

This card represents the appearance of new structures, which can be interpreted on the earthly, philosophical, spiritual, psychic, and cosmic planes. Nothing seems definitive or permanent with this card which reflects a state of constant change.

You also need to know how to measure (moderate) your actions and energy in proper proportion to what is needed in the situation so that you can reap the rewards that you desire.

Adopt a policy of putting in the right amount of effort into the right situation.

When some certain and particular situations arise, you will need to know how to rapidly and intelligently adapt yourself to the new coordinates of destiny.

Card 15: Chaos

Chaos is born from the intermarriage of arrogance, conceit, and pride.

Key for the Chaos Card

- *Be prepared for an ordeal that will cause instability in your present situation*
- *Carefully reexamine your life for a succession of errors and neglect*
- *Carefully reexamine your values, as witnessed by your actions*

Skills to be Learned from the Chaos Card

- *See the similarities instead of the differences*
- *Develop harmony, not divisiveness*
- *Develop empathy and ask for forgiveness*

Destiny for the Number 15

The destiny of the number 15 manifests as possible enslavement to materialism, glamour, luxury, and addictions to sex, drugs and alcohol. Fears are of your own making.

Numerology

The number 15 in numerology represents chaos. The esoteric meaning of the number 15 reveals that things cannot remain as they are; they are propelled toward harmony by the transformation of suffering into conscious awareness. We need to free ourselves from the slavery of attachments to leave the whirlwind of chaos.

15 Chaos

The Chaos Card

General Meaning of the Chaos Card

This card teaches that accomplishing voluntary self-mastery will show us to our path to evolution. In spite of the very negative aspects of this card, there is hope. Creative energy sleeps within the darkness of chaos. It's only a question of getting pointed in the right direction.

Symbolism of the Chaos Card

This card illustrates a bizarre kind of divided sphere containing figures and the torch of destruction.

The divided sphere in this image signifies all that divides human beings and the hatred and mistrust that resides within every nation on Earth. This sphere contains time, mortality, fate, and inflexible destiny.

Underneath the sphere is a malicious flower emitting negative energy though it.

Material concerns rule over the spiritual concerns here, shown by the central building in the image. This reflects the profound prevailing effect the primitive instinct has over intelligence and wisdom.

The figures are incarnations of slavery to the material things in life, the chaos of gruesome cravings; and the effects of arrogance, conceit, and pride.

The figures are all going in their own directions willy-nilly, oblivious to each other. This is the opposite of the laws of balance and harmony. It's obvious that the crowd has a tendency to listen to and follow the one who yells the loudest, while the discrete person is ignored. When balance is ignored, the torch of destruction takes over.

We must learn to accept and master our base instincts and desires. Just as the rider who should occupy himself with the requirements of his untended horse, we must watch over and channel the desires that spring from our physical selves, those to which we are tied all throughout this Earthly life.

Divinatory Meaning of the Chaos Card

When you (as the seeker) draw this card, you can expect a very serious trial or ordeal that will cause instability in your present situation. If you analyze it carefully, you'll see that this ordeal is the cumulative result of a succession of errors and fundamental neglect, although not necessarily due to your fault.

If it is your fault, it's obvious that you were not aware of the basic principles that can help you prepare strategies to deal with events. Your pride and ego have caused you to underestimate the opponent or adversary. You must rethink everything if you want to get out of this.

Sometimes the causes leading up to such ordeals are subtle and hard to figure out. Don't let yourself be led around by fools.

If you can find the spark inside again, a place where you recognize with humility and sincerity your unenlightened state and your blunders, you can then call on support and cosmic forgiveness. Otherwise, you'll have to pay the price.

Few people have the courage to face themselves in the mirror of self-knowledge, willing to look at all aspects of their inner lives, both the 'light' and 'dark.' They prefer to keep up their aimless activities and keep busy with their purposeless tasks.

Remember that you are the wizard of your own destiny. Don't be surprised with the arrival of your karmic results if your refuse to correct the direction of the chaos in your life.

While this card announces a trial or ordeal, it also gives you a very positive opportunity to ask for and connect to a power that is far greater than you, all the necessary energies to make it through this difficult passage.

Card 16: Tower of Dust

Ill-conceived works will surely return to the dust from which they were built.

Key for the Tower of Dust Card

- *Images and plans of grandeur may soon be shattered and fall to ruin*
- *'Returning to dust' is an important step in clearing away a poisonous situation*
- *With the right attitude, destruction may provide opportunity for growth*

Skills to be Learned from the Tower of Dust Card

- *Sincere examination of current situations*
- *Sincere willingness to let go of that which is ill-conceived*
- *Sincere introspection regarding intention and direction*

Destiny for the Number 16

The destiny of the number 16 manifests as the relativity of materialism and its consequences. Upheaval, profound change and lost illusions will lead to the revelation of inner truths.

Numerology

The number 16 in numerology reminds us that we are all subject to cosmic forces that weigh our works on the scales of cosmic justice. Those works created in odds with the cosmic plan are destined to destruction.

The Tower of Dust Card

General Meaning of the Tower of Dust Card

This card illustrates that those human works created on an ill-conceived foundation, without positive or higher elements, are destined to crumble and return to the dust from which they came. This is an important step in the Spiritual Tarot journey, for it provides many lessons along the seeker's path of spiritual growth.

Symbolism of the Tower of Dust Card

This card shows a newly constructed tower that is already beginning to crumble and fall. The man-made ropes that were intended to support the new tower, fail to do so. Even the branches from the trees that surround the tower are falling from the trees, pointing out that the structure acts as a poison within nature and the natural plan of things.

The ruin of not only of the edifice itself, but that which surrounds it highlights the ill-conceived conception and design of those who built it. The design was not based on the laws of rhythm, balance, and harmony. The ruin of the tower is the result of following self-serving desires and pride, with a total disregard of others and the planet. Those who willfully ignore and act against the good of the many are destined to incur the wrath of the cosmic forces in the court of cosmic justice.

The image also contains lightning coming down from the heavens, striking out and destroying the tower without hesitation. This again symbolizes that the ruin of such works is the equalizing cosmic force stemming from a higher sense of evaluation. All acts springing solely from egotistic or ill-willed intentions (and thus not from positive or higher realms), will all crumble and return to the dust from which they were built.

We humans should consult the higher realms (look within and discern what is best for the many, what is best for Mother Earth) before we begin construction. If we want to design and create on our own, we will succeed in the long run only insofar as we follow the cosmic laws, using the cosmic energies for the good of all. For a work to take on its own life, it must be conceived from higher energies and be designed and crafted with that same guidance.

The serene and sturdy temple below the tower represents the manifest, visible world that was conceived with principles in balance with cosmic forces. It remains intact as a legacy of its positive spiritual conception.

This card also represents the destructive and frightful forces of sex when actuated by motives other than love (by lust, callousness, selfish gratification, selfish gain, and such). When these destructive forces are generated, they exact a violent punishment far and wide.

Divinatory Meaning of the Tower of Dust Card

This card heralds the destruction of established things constructed or obtained by self-serving ambitions, pride, ego, rivalries, jealousies; or through negative or sterile (not spiritual) design. This stage of 'returning to dust' is an important and necessary step to clear away the ill-effects and poison of the current situation.

Illusions are going to be shattered, and so will the false security resulting from ill-begotten material gains or reliance upon the purely material. You must learn to let go of such things, even if you currently cherish them. Do not resist, as it would not only be in vain, but it is likely to bring even more negative energy upon you.

The tower that has been destroyed by lightening is an overwhelming catastrophe for some. Yet for others who realize the need for this unexpected change, they will know how to rebuild and start again. Thus, this card presents a great opportunity for the reversal of our mistakes.

However, there are some ordeals to be faced that are so sad or tragic that they might make your very soul moan and cry. If the current situation represents such a catastrophe for you, then hang in there, realize that there is light at the end of the tunnel. You can begin to change by beginning to try to understand your current situation differently. Look to see what you need to learn in the current situation. Try to change the way you see things, change this into an opportunity to learn and let go.

And yet other ordeals you may find can be liberating for you. For example, this card can represent the crumbling of the foundation of oppression within you, as oppression begins on the mental plane. Whether you were the oppressed or the oppressor, change the way you think about things and change the way that you perceive things. You can rebuild your psyche with positive spiritual guidance, to benefit not only you, but all society.

Do not create from negative energies and forces, or with the intention to ignore the universal cosmic laws. Cosmic judgment and retribution is especially the sure and just result for those who would apply magical forces for the attainment of self-serving, egotistical ends.

In all cases, when you draw this card you must do some serious work on self-mastery. The situation is different in each case, as it depends on your ability to comprehend these terms. You must apply yourself so that you always act out of good conscience, positive intentions, respect and dignity.

Awareness has the potential to replace the illusions in the interest of facilitating destiny's course. That is the meaning of Divine intervention.

Page intentionally left blank.

Card 17: Star

Light brings the perfect union of truth and beauty.

Key for the Star Card

- *There is definite progress in growth*
- *There is a silver lining in the dark clouds*
- *There is healing and remedies within reach*

Skills to be Learned from the Star Card

- *Refine and practice your sense of intuition*
- *Keep up hope, trust and faith*
- *Work with love and light*

Destiny for the Number 17

The destiny of the number 17 manifests as unexpected luck or success in love, business and spirituality.

Numerology

The number 17 in numerology is the sign of propagation and procreation of life. It also represents the receptivity to all abstract forces of the cosmos. The esoteric meaning of this number is active harmony.

17 Star

The Star Card

General Meaning of the Star Card

This card signifies a definite progress in growth. Symbolically speaking, the seed sown in the soil has escaped the dangers and pitfalls of a season of storms and dry spells. Its life of obscurity is over as the seed breaks through the darkness of soil into the night's air, soon to be bathed in warmth of sunlight. There is direct rapport with the night star, the symbol of creation.

When you draw this card you (as the seeker) can depend on support throughout the trials and tests you must endure. Remember, no matter how bad things seem to get, all is not lost. Healing and remedies are also brought to you with this card.

Symbolism of the Star Card

The star incorporates the perfect union of truth and beauty. The five-pointed star is lovingly surrounded by the luminous cosmic energy. The star is so powerful that it can light up the way for those who are lost or wandering, and for those who are seeking their spiritual path. Inside the top of the star, there are two love birds representing cosmic messengers bringing joyous news of hope, promise, faith, and healing.

The male and female figures shown in the middle of the star represent human consciousness in its duality of Yin and Yang. The couple is portrayed on both the spiritual and physical realms to show us that we should never become discouraged; after the rain, there is the rainbow, the promise, and the healing.

The man seeks to restore everything he approaches, symbolized by the way he is dipping his elbow into the holy waters of the vase. The water, indispensable to all life, nourishes and promotes the vegetation into blossom.

At the bottom of the image, we see a sleeping couple. The cosmic star above them has transformed their dream into reality by way of its positive energy.

Divinatory Meaning of the Star Card

With this card, the seeker perceives everything illuminated by the lucidity of truth. Everything is seen clearly, honestly. Very often, this card signals an unexpected and fortunate outcome that frees up the most complex situations. This is what is meant by the silver lining in the dark clouds.

But all is not guaranteed as a 'done deal' either. You must keep up your trust and faith, while realizing what can be accomplished given the circumstances.

The seeker need no longer fear deceitful and underhanded plots and schemes. The most important aspect to remember is hope of promises soon to be revealed.

Intuition and fair judgment should preside over the decisions that you must make. Act effectively, and always remain honorable and faithful.

This card also represents hope by showing that there exists on this planet a being who is a perfect mate for each of us, and with whom we can discover and share true love.

Card 18: Moon

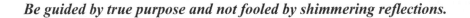

Be guided by true purpose and not fooled by shimmering reflections.

Key for the Moon Card

- *Be on guard for the lack of judgment and discernment*
- *Protect and nourish the seeds of new beginnings*
- *Don't mistake the reflection for that which it reflects*

Skills to be Learned from the Moon Card

- *Continue to develop your intuition*
- *Continue to develop your meditative practices*
- *Continue to develop the opening to your Heart*

Destiny for the Number 18

The destiny of the number 18 manifests as the subtle, the invisible, the illusion, and as imagination. Destiny reflects as the tendency to make a big deal out of something that doesn't exist or making the preverbal 'mountain out of a molehill.'

Numerology

The number 18 in numerology encourages us to let go of attachment to our ego and be guided by the true purpose of our journey. This number reminds us to stay on guard against the dangers that may threaten new beginnings.

The Moon Card

General Meaning of the Moon Card

This card reminds us of the powerful attraction of life's illusions and fantasies. It also points out the treachery and manipulation that is often interwoven within the fabric of illusion.

Don't mistake the reflection for the reality that exists right in front of you.

Be aware of the needs and feelings of other people, even though they may not be expressed openly or publically.

Try to avoid making judgments, especially when you know little about what is going on.

Symbolism of the Moon Card

This card is the symbol of woman and womanly powers; of fertility, fruitfulness, and healthy procreation. Throughout many of the classical and spiritual initiation procedures, the moon represents woman and the feminine principle in a variety of similar and different ways. Common characteristics include intuition, conception and birthing, all beginning on the spiritual plane. The moon's shape is even that of the ovum. All this symbolizes the eternal woman.

In this card, we see that the moon's shimmering light is cast on a mysterious countryside whose central image is a small temple surrounded by tall trees. The trees shown in the illustration symbolize the secrecy that typically surrounds the initiation process.

A veiled moon symbolizes concealed mystic knowledge, the development of intuition, and metaphysical secrets. The moon sheds a misty and opalescent light, making the situation gently glow. The silvery reflections cast on the ground symbolize passing through shadows and secrets, from one world into another.

The temple that is shown in the illustration, is not the divine temple, it is a barrier of sorts. The seeker must 'jump' over it, or go through it, before being able to continue on the path of spiritual growth.

There's a scorpion on the temple and two dogs close by, standing guard.

The guard dogs are protecting the threshold to the temple and blocking the path around it. The dogs are there to announce to the seeker that the lessons of this temple must be mastered first in order to continue on the journey of awareness and wisdom. Barking dogs also represent the commotion of the material world, which can distract us from our spiritual path.

And let us not forget the scorpion. If pride is what motivates the seeker to travel on this road, there will be no protection. In that case, the result will be the scorpion's sting, representing the numbness and entrapment of material illusions. The seeker has no hope of being able to continue on this path under such circumstances.

The symbolism woven throughout this card also represents the kind of initiation that women go through when developing their womanly psychic and intuitive powers. This card encompasses all activity of conception and germination, a process that develops totally veiled in mystery, including pregnancy in the physical and spiritual realms.

In this incarnation, we must cultivate all the 'seeds' we have within us (science, art, devotion, spirituality, etc.). The seeds, embryos, dreams, wishes, and concepts of this card can bear fruit with the right nourishment and growth.

Divinatory Meaning of the Moon Card

This card warns us to stay on guard against the lack of judgment or discernment in life. You are being reminded to actively develop your intuition and the sensitive side of your nature. These are very important skills you need to hone in order to avoid the pitfalls along the path.

The attractive powers of the moon signify the magnetic appeal of the mysterious, of intuition and all the psychic powers that can be cultivated in the seeker. The moon also attracts the water of the Earth, of our bodies, and within the moisture in the air we breathe. Water, in many traditions, often represents spiritual truth. The moon symbolically is attracting (drawing out) our spirit, calling to us.

The moon's light is very different from the sun's light. The sun's light is super bright, literally blindingly bright. The sun is the primordial light, light from which all other light originates. The sun's light floods the path with light.

The moon's light is much, much softer. It is a gentle, cool and mysterious light to remind us that the material world and its attractions are only a mere reflection of that primordial light. Because the moon's essence is reflected light, this card also represents mediation, negotiation, and arbitration.

When you (as the seeker) draw this card you are going through a trying period where caution, sensibility, and keen intuition are being tested. Somewhere out there, there is something going on or some disturbing event brewing. This calls for some light to be shed on the situation. But don't mistake the reflection for the real thing. When I read the Tarot for customers and they draw this card, I tell them to be careful, to watch their back and be mindful of deceitful actions by others.

When you have proved your strong conviction and good will, the cosmic energy will step in to help you, and the metaphysical principles that are represented in this card will be there to help you.

You need to know how to wait for and distinguish the most favorable and fruitful circumstances. This effort will not fail if the seeds have been sown in fertile ground and have been nourished properly. Meditation may help you in this endeavor.

Work accomplished metaphorically, under cover of darkness or in mystery, can produce either good or bad results. For you, good results will come out of your honesty and sincerity, which you must apply in all of your endeavors and if you do, you will see the bright light every day!

Page intentionally left blank.

Card 19: Sun

What you lovingly planted, nourished and cared for has now come into full bloom.

Key for the Sun Card

- *Success has been realized*
- *Love has been realized*
- *Harmony has been realized*

Skills to be Learned from the Sun Card

- *Practice mindfulness*
- *Practice sharing joy and happiness*
- *Practice random loving kindness*

Destiny for the Number 19

The destiny of the number 19 manifests as vitality, bountiful harvest, replenished luck, optimism and mastery. Destiny is reflected as inspiration to see life in a harmonious and peaceful way.

Numerology

This number represents the cycle of evolution. The esoteric meaning of this card can be seen by looking at the individual numbers in combination $1 + 9 = 10$. Then $1 + 0 = 1$. Everything returns to 1.

The Sun Card

General Meaning of the Sun Card

This card represents a major progress or advancement. The seeds were properly planted and have weathered the danger of the storms. They are now bearing fruit.

Life has come out of the mysterious waters to walk in the light and to breathe the air, like being born from the cosmic womb. Life is in direct harmony with the sun.

This card also represents joy and harmony in domestic realms and in relationships.

Symbolism of the Sun Card

This card is the symbol of the very essence of creativity and creative energy. This is not the subtle, reflected light of the moon. This is the direct and original light of the incredibly bright sun, the primordial light, the visible manifestation of creativity.

The sun is the star of life, representing all of life. The card symbolizes creative essence on the cosmic level and on the earthly plane.

The sun is the astrological symbol of the great cosmic creator and has a long history of being worshiped and honored from the earliest cultures as the creative force or divinity.

The sun symbolizes the perfection of humanity, the highest standard as a human being for both woman and man; the archetypical human, here portrayed as a youth.

The sun represents love that has been realized. And that's very important because love is the closest thing to cosmic energy. This is the sun that lights up the soul.

The sun provides both illumination and heat, two essential cosmic energies. The sun also provides splendor and abundance.

Under the sun's warmth, a happy young man is playing the flute as he strolls through a garden of flowers and wheat in bloom. He is bathed in and illuminated by the radiant light of the sun.

The bountiful flowers and wheat are all in full bloom and symbolic of peaceful coexistence, success, and great prosperity. This symbolism is reflected within all planes of existence: the material, physical, astral, and spiritual.

The flowers symbolize how intelligence and reasoning power, together with spirituality, dominate the cosmic and earthly planes. They also symbolize our mental processes being elevated into the higher realms, free from the ego's self-serving interests.

The symbolism of the flute echoes that of the flowers and wheat. The flute represents the ego transmuted into a positive tool (or servant) of spirituality. The flute also represents how the ordinary mind is raised up into higher mind, where it radiates joy as music. Universal joy and love can be touched through the doorway of the Heart (higher mind).

Divinatory Meaning of the Sun Card

When you, as the seeker, draw this card you can be assured of success. Your inspiration is centered in your heart and the heart is often symbolically compared to the sun.

You have passed through a very decisive stage, like when life came from out of the sea to begin living on the land under the light of the sun. The hard trials, ordeals and tribulations you have had to endure; all the conflicts and the struggles you have gone through are now all finished now.

And if there are any little rumbles left bothering you, don't worry. They will quickly disintegrate in the warmth of the sun. The sun has chased away all those rainy days.

This card is the epitome of hard-won success after a long struggle, victory after the grueling battle. Don't fret about lingering events because circumstances are heading in the right direction.

This is also the stage of initiation where your soul comes into a heightened state, in touch with the Divine through love and selflessness; and through the evolution of intellect, emotions, and spirituality.

Sometimes, because of the emphasis on the Heart and love, this card also signals that you have found your perfect soul-mate or love-mate.

All evolution is brought about through the energy of the sun and the creative forces it generates. All the benefits are yours as a result of your persistence, willpower, good intentions, and ability to follow through.

The most prosperous and happy future for us on Earth is through nonviolent, friendly, interactions amongst all peoples and creatures under the light of the Sun.

Page intentionally left blank.

Card 20: Awakening

With clear inner vision and right direction, you can manifest your dreams.

Key for the Awakening Card

- *The unexpected turns into reality*
- *The solution may be opposite of logic*
- *Keep an open and alert mind*

Skills to be Learned from the Awakening Card

- *See opposites as two sides of the same coin*
- *Let go of the old in order to touch the new*
- *Honor your responsibilities and your inner voice*

Destiny for the Number 20

The destiny of the number 20 manifests as self-awareness, mindfulness, fairness, balance, detachment and seeking the light.

Numerology

The number 20 in numerology is the symbol for the essence of duality. Life and death are opposites only in appearance. They actually complement each other. All death gives birth to new life, and all life prepares for death. The number 20 represents this universal cosmic law.

The Awakening Card

General Meaning of the Awakening Card

This card symbolizes an inner awakening and that another reality is now becoming possible.

This especially denotes the awakening of a spiritual life, the change in awareness that springs from deep contemplation and meditation.

It can also represent a return to the spiritual path after a cycle of being lost in the material realms.

Symbolism of the Awakening Card

This card symbolizes awakening to our spiritual essence that has been nestled asleep in the deep realms of our being. In this symbolic phase, we are learning how to die (symbolically) in the profane world to be reborn with a higher understanding of the Greater Reality. This is expressed by a kind of pseudo-death that most initiations to great wisdom entail.

This is the process whereby the seeker learns universal lessons, yet never shirks the responsibilities of life and the material existence.

The card illustrates two warriors fleeing the world of darkness, passing through the veil that separates the earthly and higher planes. The two warriors represent seekers on the spiritual path.

There are roosters on the warrior's shields, symbolizing the angelic immortality of the soul with knowledge of divine laws, moving toward a fruitful, new reality.

A large winged horse is taking flight into the cosmos, where harmony and love unite everything. The winged horse represents the alchemical influences of unity that come from these two universal forces of love and harmony.

Toward the bottom of the image there are boxes that have portraits in them, representing dreams and visualizations that will soon become reality.

This card also reminds us that our physical life on this planet is ephemeral, fleeting, and transitory. Likewise on an emotional level;

happiness, misery, joy, and sadness are here one moment and gone the next. This symbolizes the constant renewal of things, the ever revitalizing cycles of life.

Divinatory Meaning of the Awakening Card

When you (as the seeker) draw this card you are experiencing a change that is a direct result of the seeds you have sown. As the spirit blows where it will, you can add to it whenever you want. Your attitude toward this change, and the kinds of seeds you have sown, will determine how it works for you.

Radical change and upheaval can also be seen in this card, holding many surprises for you that can alter a situation drastically. You may find yourself momentarily trapped. But keep your courage, because this trapped feeling is only temporary.

Your solution, which will be a happy one, will not come from logic but from your karma, and that is often difficult to analyze. Remember your lessons, and listen to your inner voice.

Keep a positive attitude in the situations that present themselves. Take care to avoid creating a conflict between what your ordinary mind wants and the karma that would incur. Hold and practice the right attitude in order to prosper and your dreams will no longer be dreams, but will become reality.

Card 21: Supreme Achievement

You have earned the outcome of spiritually conceived success.

Key for the Supreme Achievement Card

- *Harvesting the success of earnest work performed*
- *Bearing the fruit of understanding, wholeness and cosmic rhythm*
- *Reaping the benefits from protective and nurturing cosmic forces*

Skills to be Learned from the Supreme Achievement Card

- *Continue on the path of pursuing spiritual goals*
- *Continue to observe and tame the self-centered ego*
- *Commit yourself to conscious and lucid thought and action*

Destiny for the Number 21

The destiny of the number 21 manifests as achievement, great vision, fulfillment of work well-done, all without the hindrances of the self-centered ego.

Numerology

The number 21 is a number of perfection and eternity. Eternity carries within it great positivity, success, attainment, and affirmation. The number 21, as represented by 3 x 7, symbolizes the three phases of human life: from birth to coming-of-age at 21; from 21 to middle age at 42; and from 42 to the "grand climacteric" at 63. The number 21 also represents the last phase in the major spiritual lessons to be learned along the path with the Spiritual Tarot.

21 Supreme Achievement

The Supreme Achievement Card

General Meaning of the Supreme Achievement Card

This card represents the perfect harvest as you reap what you have sown during the course of the last 20 Spiritual Tarot lessons. If the process went well during these 20 lessons, the present reward will be supreme achievement and the most dazzling, gratifying fulfillment.

This is reflected as satisfaction, total contentment and even bliss, as the result of attaining the accomplishments you desired. All of this leads to ultimate understanding, wholeness and cosmic rhythm.

This card represents complete victory after all of the demanding trials, tribulations, ordeals, and tests that you have endured and passed through along this difficult initiation journey.

Symbolism of the Supreme Achievement Card

This is a very powerful card, representing supreme achievement, affirmation and attunement with the cosmic rhythm. Your work has been recognized and the results will go beyond all aspirations.

Complete success is announced as a crowning glory to your actions and accomplishments that have been carried out with awareness, skill, and soulful dignity. This card signals the outcome of spiritually conceived success.

This card symbolizes harmonic balance within the material realm, experienced as realized projects on Earth that are infused with cosmic inspiration and design. An example of such a realized project is illustrated by the temple in the card.

The temple represents cosmic creative energy in action, movement that energizes the thriving gestation process. It's the divine rhythm that controls all action that's on its way to accomplishment. The steps to the temple symbolize that hard yet finally successful journey.

The young woman symbolizes the Universal Cosmic Mother. She is bent in a gesture of congratulations. She touches her hand to the seeker, who has now become a mature initiate, transformed from the young student that she/he once was in the beginning. The seeker now contemplates the brilliant achievements brought about by her/his efforts.

The shield depicts a horse and a lion. The horse represents freedom from materialistic greed and the lion represents courage and strength. This shield represents the protection that comes with pursuing positive spiritual goals. The bird is a cosmic messenger and represents the spiritual evolution and the immortal soul.

This card also represents the perfect union expressed on all three planes as perfect harmony of desire, intellect, and spirituality. It can also signify a perfect and durable union in relationships founded in love.

Divinatory Meaning of the Supreme Achievement Card

In the beginning you were the student who was inexperienced, and now you have succeeded in passing through all the initiation stages to win inner freedom.

You have passed from the illusion of the separateness of the self-centered ego, to the awareness of Divine connection within all things in the universe. The universe is not a collection of individuals; it is One. The Heart within every human being, within every living being, connects each of us with all others. All are an interconnected part of the energy that is the web-of-life, that is the universe.

Having gradually integrated and blended both material life and the spiritual dimension, you, the initiate, are filled with ecstasy. All these forces are within you, and they radiate from you, representing a gathering together and a concurrence of all the wisdom and experience you have attained.

You are like a theater goer, aware of the characters and circumstance in front of you, but no longer bound by the trappings or attachments of what goes on. And even though it's a world whose urgency, purpose, and methods you understand, you as the initiate, will have little need to take public forum. Belonging to a group who find solace within, you have begun to prefer silence, humility, and modesty as methods of both communion and communication.

The spiritual energy of awareness accompanies you with all its power as long as you pursue a virtuous and spiritual goal. Commit yourself to conscious and lucid acts, with excellent intentions, without hindrance from the ego. Great results will follow.

This card also encourages all those who are searching for their soul mate because this is a very promising and favorable time for that meeting. Along the path of initiation, we sometimes find our counterpart or complement, present during this step of the journey. And there may be more than one soul-mate or love-mate for us in this world. But, in the event that you don't run across your complement in the manifest world, realize that this complement is actually within you. Find out who you are by seeking within.

You are in the best phase of your spiritual journey. You have received your graduation from the 'cosmic university'!

Be ready for life without regret!

Page intentionally left blank.

Card: Fool

Look for warning signs of danger both within yourself and in the world around.

Key for the Fool Card

- *Immersion in material concerns and blind to perception*
- *What appears dangerous may be a cosmic warning to take heed*
- *Tap into your power of discernment and intuition*

Skills to be Learned from the Fool Card

- *Realize the falsehood of 'ignorance is bliss'*
- *Realize the emptiness of vanity, egotism, and pride*
- *Realize the darkness that shrouds illumination and clarity*

Destiny for the Number 22

The destiny of the number 22 manifests as unlimited possibilities and potential that may be taken for granted and misused.

Numerology

In some Tarot decks (including this one), the number 22 does not appear on the card at all because these systems consider the card as zero (without any numerical value). Zero is the number of imbecility and stupidity. Zero is nothing.

The Fool Card

General Meaning of the Fool Card

This card represents the dangers facing the human who is unconscious and unaware of cosmic laws. This person moves through life with vanity, egotism, and false pride. He thinks he is invulnerable because he can't see the rampant warnings of the perils, risks, and threats that await him.

The Fool lives as though the phrase 'ignorance is bliss' is actually true.

Symbolism of the Fool Card

This card shows a man with a blank expression, mightily waving a stick in the left hand, while shaking his right fist as though he could yield great power. The sun is in mid-eclipse above the scene. The sea is raging in front of the man, and a hyena waits patiently on the side of the road.

The expressionless face of the foolish man symbolizes an individual who is wholly immersed in material concerns, devoid of intuition, blind to any perception of the higher power and its manifestations. He is ignorant to anything that exists beyond immediate satisfaction.

The man's little, thin, and ineffective stick and his empty shaking fist symbolize the insignificance of vanity, egotism, and pride.

The perils, risks, threats, and warnings that await the man are symbolized by the sea and the hyena.

The hyena also represents nothingness, anti-being, and the brutal and cruel annihilation to all who would approach it without caution and awareness.

The roaring sea additionally symbolizes the mental prison we plunge into and drown in when we refuse to listen to the inner voice that beckons us home.

The eclipse of the sun represents a darkness that shrouds illumination and clarity, and doubt overtaking faith.

The Fool is a symbol of the 'sleeping' majority within humanity who have yet to discover that true happiness, peace and meaningful purpose, lie outside of society's customary rewards of money, fame, and power.

Everything that is created by the sole hand of man, devoid of spiritual energy, will remain in the realm of a fragile, unstable, and perishable relativity.

Laziness and self-satisfaction is represented here.

Divinatory Meaning of the Fool Card

When you (as the seeker) draw this card, you should look around for warning signs of impending danger. The hyena, in spite of its menacing appearance, shows a way to flee this situation if you have a sudden flash of awareness or intuition. The presence of the hyena thus is a cosmic warning to take heed.

Tap into your power of discernment and intuition. If you do so, you will benefit from the positive energies that this card also offers. These energies contain the forces of extremes; those forces that can blow up that which exists and those forces that can help establish order.

But if you are ruled by false pride and the self-centered ego, you will remain stuck in your ill-fated satisfaction and materialistic greed. This materialism can be an influential force, but we must learn to see clearly through it. We must act, not react.

This card reveals a phase in your journey in which you may feel hindered in self-reflection, trapped under the illusions that work against you, and blocked from necessary spiritual growth. Don't forget that the power of thought dominates all actions. Efforts to direct your thinking in positive and constructive directions may be difficult, but you must do it. You must have a clear goal. If you don't know where you're headed, not even a tailwind will help you get there.

If you draw this card and you are not the Fool, you may be receiving a warning that you are surrounded by fools. They will flatter, deceive, and trick you, and eventually lead you astray. Stay away from fools! They prevent you from continuing on the path of growth.

Be very careful about the company you keep. We unwittingly absorb negative energies, and this can be fatal to your desire for clarity.

Seek out instead those who actively pursue a spiritual path, brothers and sisters with whom you share common goals and direction. Spiritual community provides shared strength to all who contribute.

This card could thus be a warning to you that you need to retire from the chaos of the world and retreat into meditation and self-reflection.

This card is the final test that the student must pass in order to become an initiate. You must understand that you can never think that you have arrived at some near-perfect state.

Spiritual work on the earthly plane is never really completed, it is a process. It is a journey, not a destination. The journey is more of a spiral than a straight line. We pass through the same lessons again and again, but each time we learn finer and deeper aspects of these lessons.

Continue to develop the connection to your spiritual nature that resides in the very center of your being. Divine love waits for you there.

Concentrate on the knowledge you have gained and have faith in your destiny. But be very careful. If you don't apply the gifts that you've worked so hard to develop over the course of these lessons, you may fall hard and fast into the trap of illusion. You will pay a big price if you do not heed this warning in this lifetime or the next.

Page intentionally left blank.

About the Author

Marie-Claire Wilson has over 35 years of experience and studies in the divinatory arts, especially as a clairvoyant, intuitive consultant, and Tarot reader in France, Switzerland, and the United States. She also teaches the divinatory arts, mainly the Tarot, having given classes over the years in Paris, Toulouse, and Marseilles, France; in Geneva, Switzerland; and in the United States, where she currently resides.

The divinatory arts are a gift that runs in Marie-Claire's family. Her great-grandmother was a very well-known medium just outside of Marseilles, France. It was through her great-grandmother that Marie-Claire was first introduced to the crystal ball, Tarot decks and the other 'tools of the trade'. Marie-Claire's mother and aunt also have 'the gift' but they don't actively practice with it.

Marie-Claire was born in Marseilles, the second largest city in France. She earned a B.P. (in philosophy and literature) in France and after graduating from the Conservatoire de musique et de déclamation de Marseille (University of Theatrical Arts of Marseilles), she performed as a professional actress for several years. Upon her father's insistence, she also obtained a degree in Business International (Monaco).

As a young adult Marie-Claire moved to Switzerland where she met Mag. Mag became Marie-Claire's mentor and spent years helping Marie-Claire develop her intuitive and physic abilities. Mag also introduced Marie-Claire to spirituality and helped her begin her spiritual journey.

Marie-Claire changed careers in order to completely devote herself as a serious student of the spiritual, psychic, and divinatory arts. She continued her metaphysical studies in various places within Europe.

Marie-Claire was selected as the best reader at the 'Festival of Clairvoyance' in 1987 in Geneva, Switzerland. She was interviewed on a number of radio shows in Paris and Monaco, where she conducted Tarot readings with callers. She has participated in many clairvoyance conferences in Europe and the United States. In 1997 Marie-Claire was featured speaker in the International World Tarot Congress in Chicago.

Marie-Claire was featured in three television shows in the United States, two on local Atlanta broadcast and one on the Weather Channel with nationwide broadcast. She is an active writer and contributor to new age publications, having written over 1000 articles and conducted over 150 interviews during the last 15 years.

Marie-Claire continues to teach the Tarot and the divinatory arts, while maintaining a thriving business as an intuitive consultant in the Washington DC area, where she lives with her husband and 4-legged child (little dog). Her clients include people from all walks of life including soccer moms, doctors, lawyers, judges, law enforcement officers, national security officers, teachers, hair stylists, engineers, work -at-home parents, corporate officers, government employees, politicians, celebrities and many others.

For more information, visit Marie-Claire's web site.

http://www.marie-claire.tv